Made
According to
Pattern

Made According to Pattern

A Study of the Tabernacle
in the Wilderness

by

Charles W. Slemming

Author of:
These Are The Garments
He Leadeth Me
Thus Shalt Thou Serve

CHRISTIAN ❖ LITERATURE ❖ CRUSADE
Fort Washington, Pennsylvania 19034

CHRISTIAN LITERATURE CRUSADE
U.S.A.
P.O. Box 1449, Fort Washington, PA 19034

GREAT BRITAIN
51 The Dean, Alresford, Hants. SO24 9BJ

AUSTRALIA
P.O. Box 419M, Manunda, QLD 4879

NEW ZEALAND
10 MacArthur Street, Feilding

ISBN 0-87508-565-2

Preface

OF all Old Testament studies, each holding its own attraction, and of all typology, with its fascinating facets of truth, I find there is no subject more absorbing and no theme more complete in its truth than that of "the tabernacle."

It was back in 1928, when preaching at Faversham, that I first saw a model of a tabernacle and became interested. Not long after that I built my first model and began to study the subject. I eventually built three different models, had one created by an engineer, and then developed a very large flannelgraph on the topic.

1928 is a long time back, but over those thirty-five years my interest in this subject has never waned; in fact, it has grown. And when I give a series of studies or lectures on the matter, it always grips my soul with a new sense of wonder and beauty as it reveals the Lord, the Church, and the will of the Lord concerning that Church.

It was in 1938 that I responded to the request of many people to put these lectures on the tabernacle into print, and thus it was that *Made According to Pattern* came onto the market.

It is with a rejoicing heart and thanksgiving to the Lord that I write this preface for the sixth printing. In doing so I can recommend the book with confidence, inasmuch as it is now considered a standard work. It is being used as a textbook for students in a number of Bible colleges in the United States, and has found its way into many other countries around the world, carrying blessing wherever it goes.

This edition of *Made According to Pattern* has been published in the popular paperback form to keep it in a price range that will enable it to have wider circulation. I hope that many who enjoy reading the book may in the future have an opportunity to attend some of the lectures and see the models.

So I prayerfully send out this edition, trusting that the Lord will put the seal of His blessing upon it.

Yours because His,
C. W. Slemming.
1963

Editor's Note
Estimates of the monetary value of the various items fabricated from gold, silver, bronze, etc., are those made by the author in 1963.

Contents

List of Illustrations

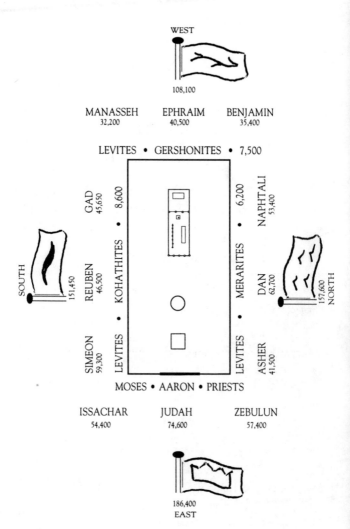

DIAGRAM 1.
PLAN OF THE ENCAMPMENT OF THE CHILDREN OF ISRAEL.

CHAPTER 1

Introduction

Exodus 25:1–9. Exodus 35. Hebrews 8.

Then the Lord spoke to Moses, saying: "Speak to the children of Israel, that they bring Me an offering. From everyone who gives it willingly with his heart you shall take My offering. And this is the offering which you shall take from them: gold, silver, and bronze; blue and purple and scarlet yarn, fine linen thread, and goats' hair; rams' skins dyed red, badger skins, and acacia wood; oil for the light, and spices for the anointing oil and for the sweet incense; onyx stones, and stones to be set in the ephod and in the breastplate. And let them make Me a sanctuary, that I may dwell among them. According to all that I show you, that is, the pattern of the tabernacle and the pattern of all its furnishings, just so you shall make it." (Ex. 25:1–9)

THE BOOK OF EXODUS falls naturally into two distinct sections, the first being historical and the second legislative. Chapters 1 to 19 are occupied with the history of a people in bondage, the birth of a leader, their emancipation and journeyings as far as Sinai. Following these chapters come twenty-one more that outline the giving and putting into action of a threefold law, namely: the moral, the civil, and the ceremonial. The moral law controlled individual life, the civil law governed national life, and the ceremonial law ordered religious life.

Concerning the book as a whole, but particularly in regard to the historical section, it has been recently asserted that outside evidence of Israel's stay in Egypt and of their journeyings in the wilderness is practically nil and certainly very conflicting. But why need we get agitated as to how they crossed the Red Sea and where? The fact is they *did*, or the Bible cannot be believed. Why argue regarding the specific site of Sinai? Should we not be more concerned with the law given there and the God who came there to dwell in the midst of a people whom He had chosen for Himself? The greatest blessing of the Word is found not so much in external evidence— although we thank God for it—but in its eternal truth which can be appropriated by simple faith in its divine authorship.

The introductory chapters of Exodus certainly constitute a romantic and thrilling story—about God's great deliverance; but is it not a wonderful and inspiring continuation when, halfway through the book, we discover that God was desiring to *dwell* with His people? Thus we come to the words of chapter 25:8: "And let them make Me a sanctuary, that I may dwell among them." It is this *tabernacle*, with its priesthood and offerings, upon which we desire to meditate. This book will deal only with the tabernacle.

May we first be permitted to answer the critic, whom we meet so often, because in so doing we shall better understand the reason for spending so much time on this subject.

There are a large number of people who say that these things have long since been done away with— so forget them! But is that a valid reason for ignoring them? Jesus did not. For "beginning at Moses [the tabernacle, law, etc.] and all the Prophets, *He expounded* to them in *all* the Scriptures the things concerning Himself" (Lk. 24:27). Herein is our authority for studying these things now. Christ said that *He* was in them; so we are not rash, unscriptural, or out of date in dealing with Old Testament truths. Moreover, the importance of the subject can be readily seen when we bear in mind that "all Scripture is given by inspiration of God, and is profitable for doctrine, for reproof, for correction, for instruction in righteousness" (2 Tim. 3:16). God gave only two chapters to the subject of the creation of the cosmos, earth, and all its creatures, including mankind; but He set apart no less than fifty chapters to this most entrancing subject under our consideration. If, then, God has inspired all for our profit, He must have seen much more profit in the tabernacle than in details about the earth's formation.

The allotment of these fifty chapters is:

Exodus	13 chapters
Numbers	13 chapters
Leviticus	18 chapters
Deuteronomy.	2 chapters
Hebrews	4 chapters,

and other references.

In addition, Paul in his day made reference to the tabernacle.

People casually say, "Oh, these things are only shadows." Have we a right to say "only" to anything in the purposes of God? True it is that they were shadows, but trace any shadow with the light before you and you will arrive at the substance; on the other hand, turn your back on the light and you will surely get away from the realities. What we purpose to do is to consider these shadows with the light of the Holy Spirit and divine revelation before us until . . .

> "The things of earth will grow strangely dim,
>   In the light of His glory and grace."

The first question we should ask ourselves is: "What is a tabernacle?" According to the dictionary, it is "a temporary dwelling place." This may be interesting to trace out. God said, "Let them make Me a sanctuary, that I may *dwell* among them" (Ex. 25:8). Was it temporary? Yes, just for 400 years. Then the temple was built, which was for the kingdom period—after which Christ took up His abode in the heart of each believer. "Do you not know that you are the temple of God and that the Spirit of God dwells in you?" (1 Cor. 3:16). Our body is likewise referred to as a "tabernacle"—a tent—because it is the temporal abode of our immortal soul (2 Cor. 5:1–4).

If we meditate on the term "church" in the same way, we learn that it is an *ekklesia,* meaning "that which is called out." The church, then, is a community of *people* and, strictly speaking, the word "church" should never be applied to a building. The church is a called-out company of people who meet together temporarily in a tabernacle until by and by they meet God and take up their abode with Him forever.

Another question often asked is: "Why was the tabernacle built?" The same verse answers this question: "that I may dwell among them." I once heard it said that the tabernacle was "a kindergarten lesson to teach an illiterate people something about God." No, it was not a paltry lesson; it was a vital part of their national life, and the people were not so illiterate. Moses never designed a tabernacle and invited God to it, as this statement would suggest; it was God who conceived the plan and instructed man to build it because He had a desire to dwell among His chosen people. This purpose of God thus to dwell develops as we travel on through the Scriptures. The God who dwelt in the tabernacle and the temple in the old dispensation found an abode in Christ during His life on earth. "God was in Christ reconciling the world to Himself" (2 Cor. 5:19), and so He was called "Immanuel . . . God with us" (Matt. 1:23). Now in this present age He is abiding in us: "He who is in you is greater than he who is in the world" (1 Jn. 4:4b).

One final question: "How was the tabernacle to be built?" This question will take the rest of our study to answer. Suffice it here to say that it was "according to the pattern." It was made according to the pattern of things in the heavenlies, things which were revealed to Moses while on the Mount. It paralleled, so it would appear, the pattern that was later shown to John while he was on the island of Patmos, for we find in the book of Revelation an altar of sacrifice (Rev. 6:9); a sea of glass (Rev. 4:6); seven golden lampstands (Rev. 1:12); the golden altar (Rev. 8:3); hidden manna (Rev. 2:17); and the ark of His covenant (Rev. 11:19). Repeatedly, in both Exodus and Hebrews, the Lord said, "See that you make it according to the pattern." God was very particular in planning it; no doubt Moses was scrupulous in the building of it; and ought not we to be careful in the understanding of it? According to Exodus 31:1–3, God anointed Bezaleel with the Spirit of God for all manner of workmanship. He will also anoint us with the Holy Spirit for the true understanding and interpretation of these things. Every detail holds its spiritual significance and lesson, hence the carefulness.

It was made from the freewill offerings of the people. "Speak to the children of Israel, that they bring Me an offering. From everyone who gives it willingly with his heart you shall take My offering" (Ex. 25:2). To this appeal the people responded so that the chosen workmen came to Moses, saying, "The people bring much more than enough for the service of the work which the Lord commanded us to do." So Moses issued a command, and a proclamation was circulated throughout the camp: "Let neither man nor woman do any more work for the offering of the sanctuary." Thus the people were restrained from bringing any more, for the material they had was sufficient for all the work to be done—indeed too much (Ex. 36:5–7). But from where did these delivered slaves get such quantities of gold, silver, brass, spices, precious stones, etc.? We are told that they plundered the Egyptians. God gave to them so that they might give to God, and when the opportunity came they were not slow in responding. Here lies our very first lesson, and a very important one too. Giving is a privilege, giving is a responsibility, giving is part of worship—but the gift must be given willingly, for the Lord loves a *cheerful* giver. We are only stewards for God. If He has given to us, it is for the very purpose that we might give to Him.

It was a giving that left no one out. The gold, silver, spices, and precious stones came from the rich; the blue, purple and scarlet yarn, and the bronze, from another class; the goats' hair from the poor. For those who had no substance to offer, there was the giving of skill and labor. This, too, was varied. Woodworkers, metalworkers, weavers and embroiderers—all had a share in the great work. And so it is in the work of the Lord today. Each one of us plays our part, remembering this one thing: when God gave, He gave His best. Christ gave His all; He held nothing in reserve. Lord, help us to do the same!

"What shall I bring to the Saviour?
What shall I lay at His feet?
I have no glittering jewels,
Gold, or frankincense so sweet.

"Gifts to the Saviour I'm bringing,
Love's richest treasure to lay
Low at His feet with rejoicing
Ere yonder sunset today.

"What shall I bring to the Saviour?
  Lips His dear praises to sing,
  Feet that will walk in the pathway
  Leading to Jesus, our King.

"What shall I bring to the Saviour?
  Love that is purest and best,
  Life in its sweetness and beauty,
  All for His service so blest."

· CHAPTER 2 ·

The Fellowship of the Tabernacle

HAVE YOU ever asked yourself the question: "Why did God create me?" Such questions are good because they provoke thought. Thought demands investigation, and investigation should drive us to the Word of God. The great purpose for which God created man was that he might have fellowship with Him.

This thought, like many others, is conveyed throughout the Bible. Most of the great themes of doctrine find their birth in the early chapters of Scripture and their full consummation in the closing chapters. With regard to this subject of fellowship, we learn that God not only desires it but constantly moves nearer to the heart of man. Strangely, however, man is not as anxious to have fellowship with God as God longs for it with man.

With this in mind, we learn that the tabernacle is but one cog in the wheel of communion, one movement in the opening of the beautiful flower of fellowship, one place of residence in a series of dwelling places.

1. God in the Garden. "And they heard the voice of the Lord God walking in the garden in the cool of the day . . ." (Gen. 3:8). The God who made man and placed him in the garden was the God who came down to that man, walked with him and talked to him. We are not told how long this fellowship continued. It was possibly a long time, until the day arrived when God came to Adam but Adam did not come to God. Instead, Adam tried to hide from God—a thing man cannot do. What had happened? Sin had come into the heart of man, sin that separated man from his Maker; but be it known that, while sin had broken that fellowship, it had not altered the desire of God for it, not for a moment of time. Man may turn his back, but with God there is no shadow of turning. We find, therefore, that God sought to establish that fellowship wherever and whenever the opportunity afforded. He walked with Enoch, He talked to Abram, He communed with Moses and others, until we find . . .

2. God in the Tabernacle. And the Lord spoke to Moses, saying, "Let them make Me a sanctuary, that I may dwell among them" (Ex. 25:8). It is to be observed that the narrative does not suggest that Moses proposed building a tabernacle and then inviting God to occupy it, but contrariwise. God, who had looked down in love and pity upon these people, and had brought them out of the bondage of Egypt, and was then leading them toward a promised land, desired not only to direct them but also to "dwell" with them. Therefore He instructed Moses to build this tabernacle and to set it up in the midst of the camp—just as a Bedouin chieftain would have his tent pitched in the midst of his encampment. The tabernacle, as we shall learn, was a portable, temporary dwelling place. These people were pilgrims living in tents, moving from place to place. The idea of the tabernacle, therefore, was that God had become a "pilgrim" with pilgrims and occupied a "tent" with tent-dwellers—or, God came right down to where man was that he might have fellowship with Him. "There I will meet with you, and I will speak with you . . ." (Ex. 25:22).

3. God in Solomon's Temple. "The cloud filled the house of the Lord, so that the priests could not continue ministering because of the cloud; for the glory of the Lord filled the house of the Lord" (1 Kings 8:10–11). The pages of history tell of the ending of the pilgrimage, of the people entering the land of Palestine and then occupying it. Pilgrimage gives place to residency, wanderings to settlement, desert to fruitful fields, and tents to houses. They were now an established people. They had become a kingdom. They had a king.

It was then that David observed that though he dwelt in a house of cedar, God still dwelt symbolically inside tent curtains (the tabernacle). David's request was that he should build a house worthy of His God. While God appreciated David's desire, yet He could not permit David to build such a temple because he was a man of war. Nonetheless, God gave His consent to the change, but it was to be David's son who would build the temple. So Solomon came to the throne, and with great magnificence and with tremendous costliness he built the temple. Then, on the great day of dedication the glory of the Lord came down and filled the place.

God was now in the midst of His people—occupying a permanent house in the midst of a permanent people. Here God and man met in fellowship and communion. In this place man could pray and worship, and God had promised to hear. Both the tabernacle and the temple were wonderful in their detail and structure. The one was a portable building, the other a permanent structure.

As generations progressed, however, the people of Israel turned their backs on God. Many indulged in idolatry. God's anger was kindled against them, so that Nebuchadnezzar, King of Babylon, came up against Jerusalem and destroyed it. The temple was demolished. The furnishings of gold and bronze were carried away, and the people became exiles in a strange country. This is known as the Babylonian Captivity.

After seventy years there was a return of the people under the hands of Zerubbabel, Ezra and Nehemiah.

4. God in Zerubbabel's Temple. "Now the temple was finished. . . . Then the children of Israel . . . celebrated the dedication of this house of God with joy" (Ezra 6:15–16). This temple was poor and insignificant compared with the one built by Solomon, so much so that "many of the priests and Levites and heads of the fathers' houses, who were old men, who had seen the first temple, wept with a loud voice when the foundation of this temple was laid before their eyes" (Ezra 3:12). Poor as this building was by comparison, God was pleased to receive it and to take up His abode with His people again.

God only accepts the best, and He accepted this because it was the best the nation could offer Him, seeing they were an impoverished people who had recently returned from exile.

From the Old Testament one moves to the New Testament and is soon introduced to . . .

5. Herod's Temple. But God was not in this temple. As the Bible does not give an account of its construction, it is necessary to turn to history. From Josephus we learn that Herod suggested that the Jewish people should give him the right to replace the temple built by Zerubbabel by another which he would build—one that would be more worthy of the name of their God and of their worship. This suggestion became a fact.

It is known that Herod was a wicked man and a cruel king. He had no genuine faith in God and no true interest in the Jewish people. So the question arises: Why did Herod want to build this temple? The answer is that Herod knew that he was a much-hated man and that when death came he would soon be forgotten. Scripture says: "There will be no prospect for the evil man; the lamp of the wicked will be put out" (Prov. 24:20). Therefore he conceived the idea of building a temple for the perpetuation of his name—and in this he succeeded. If this be true, then Herod's Temple was not in the will of God.

This thought can be strengthened by the fact that in Herod's Temple there was no ark of the covenant and no *Shekinah* glory. Jesus ministered only in the outer court. He had no access to the inner sanctuaries. God was not there. The temple had been made to become a den of thieves in the hardness and coldness of its ritualism.

Someone will say: "Did not Jesus refer to it as His Father's house?" What the Lord said was: "My [Father's] house shall be called a house of prayer, but you have made it a den of thieves." He stated what it *should* be, but obviously it was not. This corruption could have dated back to the time when Herod, with wrong motive, built the temple.

The reason why God was not in this temple was that it was not in His will. He had never required its construction. God had fellowshiped with man through the offerings and the sacrifices of the temple of the Old Testament, but He was moving away from ritual to reality, from shadow to substance, and had at this time provided His own temple, for . . .

6. God Was in Christ. "That is, that God was in Christ reconciling the world to Himself, not imputing their trespasses to them . . ." (2 Cor. 5:19). "Jesus answered and said to them, 'Destroy this temple, and in three days I will raise it up.' But He was speaking of the temple of His body" (John 2:19, 21).

His name was Immanuel, which means "God with us." In the person of Christ, in the form of man God was getting nearer to man in fellowship. While forms and ceremonies remained cold and inflexible, Jesus was moved with compassion. He had feelings and understanding. He was tempted in all points as we are. We have said that God occupies only the best: here was a sinless life, here was the perfect Man.

Each temple was short-lived. The tabernacle wore out and was replaced by the temple. Solomon's

Temple was destroyed by Nebuchadnezzar. Zerubbabel's Temple was superceded by Herod's. Herod's Temple was destroyed by Titus. The temple of Christ's body was destroyed by the Romans when they nailed It to a tree.

Now another temple comes into being.

7. God in You. "Do you not know that you are the temple of God and that the Spirit of God dwells in you?" (1 Cor. 3:16). "For you are the temple of the living God. As God has said: 'I will dwell in them, and walk among them. I will be their God, and they shall be My people'" (2 Cor. 6:16b). "Christ in you, the hope of glory" (Col. 1:27b). If this be true—and it is—then our bodies should be kept sweet and clean, and pure and holy. The realization that our bodies are the temples of God should remove from our hearts and minds all doubtful and questionable things, for God dwells only in the best. Oh, the wonder of this truth!

God has surely come very near to man when He takes up an occupancy within us. Meditate on it, beloved! It should lead to a life of full surrender and of holiness.

But God can occupy our bodies for only a limited time because these bodies are subject to death. This temple will be destroyed by the last enemy, which is death.

This leads us right into the full consummation of this fellowship:

8. God with Man and Man with God. "For we know that if our earthly house, this tent, is destroyed, we have a building from God, a house not made with hands, eternal in the heavens" (2 Cor. 5:1). This is the only temple that is eternal. It knows no end.

We started with God coming down to earth to fellowship with man. We end with man going up to God in heaven to dwell with Him forevermore.

> "Forever with the Lord,
>   Amen, so let it be.
>   Life from the dead is in that word,
>   'Tis immortality.
>   Here in the body pent,
>   Absent from Him I roam,
>   Yet nightly pitch my moving tent
>   A day's march nearer home."

Chapter 3

Relative Positions

Exodus 26:18–22. Numbers 2 and 3.

And the Lord spoke to Moses and Aaron, saying: "Everyone of the children of Israel shall camp by his own standard, beside the emblems of his fathers' house; they shall camp some distance from the tabernacle of meeting. On the east side, toward the rising of the sun, those of the standard of the forces with Judah shall camp according to their armies; and Nahshon the son of Amminadab shall be the leader of the children of Judah." And his army was numbered at seventy-four thousand six hundred. "Those who camp next to him shall be the tribe of Issachar, and Nethaneel the son of Zuar shall be the leader of the children of Issachar." And his army was numbered at fifty-four thousand four hundred. "Then shall come the tribe of Zebulun, and Eliab the son of Helon shall be the leader of the children of Zebulun." And his army was numbered at fifty-seven thousand four hundred. "All who were numbered according to their armies of the forces with Judah, one hundred and eighty-six thousand four hundred—these shall break camp first.

"On the south side shall be the standard of the forces with Reuben according to their armies, and the leader of the children of Reuben shall be Elizur the son of Shedeur." And his army was numbered at forty-six thousand five hundred. "Those who camp next to him shall be the tribe of Simeon, and the leader of the children of Simeon shall be Shelumiel the son of Zurishaddai." And his army was numbered at fifty-nine thousand three hundred. "Then shall come the tribe of Gad, and the leader of the children of Gad shall be Eliasaph the son of Reuel." And his army was numbered at forty-five thousand six hundred and fifty. "All who were numbered according to their armies of the forces with Reuben, one hundred and fifty-one thousand four hundred and fifty—they shall be the second to break camp. Then the tabernacle of meeting shall move out with the camp of the Levites in the middle of the camps; as they camp, so they shall move out, everyone in his place, by their standards.

"On the west side shall be the standard of the forces with Ephraim according to their armies, and the leader of the children of Ephraim shall be Elishama the son of Ammihud." And his army was numbered at forty thousand five hundred. "Next to him shall be the tribe of Manasseh, and the leader of the children of Manasseh shall be Gamaliel the son of Pedahzur." And his army was numbered at thirty-two thousand two hundred. "Then shall come the tribe of Benjamin, and the leader of the children of Benjamin shall be Abidan the son of Gideoni." And his army was numbered at thirty-five thousand four hundred. "All who were numbered according to their armies of the forces with Ephraim, one hundred and eight thousand one hundred—they shall be the third to break camp.

The standard of the forces with Dan shall be on the north side according to their armies, and the leader of the children of Dan shall be Ahiezer the son of Ammishaddai." And his army was numbered at sixty-two thousand seven hundred. "Those who camp next to him shall be the tribe of Asher, and the leader of the children of Asher shall be Pagiel the son of Ocran." And his army was numbered at forty-one thousand five hundred. "Then shall come the tribe of Naphtali, and the leader of the children of Naphtali shall be Ahira the son of Enan. And his army was numbered at fifty-three thousand four hundred. All who were numbered of the forces with Dan, one hundred and fifty-seven thousand six hundred—they shall break camp last, with their standards."

These are the ones who were numbered of the children of Israel by their fathers' houses. All who were numbered according to their armies of the forces were six hundred and three thousand five hundred and fifty. But the Levites were not numbered among the children of Israel, just as the Lord commanded Moses. Thus the children of Israel did according to all that the Lord commanded Moses; so they camped by their standards and so they broke camp, each one by his family, according to their fathers' houses. (Num. 2:1–34)

THERE ARE several interesting and instructive things to be gained by meditating upon the position of the tabernacle and its furniture, and of their general relationship, whether stationary or on the move.

1. Its Relation to the Camp. The tabernacle always found its position in the very midst of the camp. You will notice in Diagram 1* exactly how the various tribes were arranged. The tents were pitched at a distance from the building. Judah, with Issachar and Zebulun, on the east numbered 186,400 men. On the south was the encampment of Reuben, Simeon, and Gad, under the standard of Reuben,

* See page 10.

numbering 151,450 men. At the back of the tabernacle, westward, was Ephraim, together with his associates Manasseh and Benjamin. They totaled 108,100
men. To the north was Dan, accompanied by Asher
and Naphtali, making another 157,600 men, thus
bringing the totality of men of twenty years and upwards to 603,550, not including the tribe of Levi.
This tribe, divided into three families or clans, pitched
between the tabernacle and the camp, a clan on
each side. 8,600 of the clan of Kohath occupied the
south side. The Gershonites were on the west, in
number 7,500, and on the north were the Merarites,
another 6,200. At the front, or east, were the tents
of a subdivision of Kohathites: Moses the leader,
Aaron the High Priest, and the sons of Aaron, the
priests. Then right in the center was God.

God is, and always has been, a God of order. God
never did mean for man to please himself. Christ did
not do so—He came to do His Father's will. The
apostle said: "Though He was a Son, yet He learned
obedience by the things which He suffered" (Heb.
5:8). It is the desire of the Lord that we submit to
His plans and purposes, "You in your small corner
and I in mine." By obedience to this plan, we should
certainly find the Christian life a far, far happier one.

The significance and beauty of this arrangement
is better understood if we were to consider a Bedouin
company moving about the desert. Every camp has
its sheik or chieftain. We see him leading the way
on his camel or Arabian steed, and carrying in his
hand his spear, which varies from fifteen to twenty
feet in length. When the chieftain wants to settle

his camp for a while he just plants his spear into the ground. That is the sign of rest. His servants will immediately erect their master's tent behind the spear and then pitch their own tents around in a circle or circles, depending on the size of the camp. The sheik dwells in the midst of his people. When he desires to move on, he removes his spear and rides forth. So we see the picture: Jacob's descendants are a company of about a million and a half people wandering through the wilderness. Their chieftain is Jehovah God, whose spear is a pillar of cloud and fire. When it moves, they move; when it stays, they stay. His servants, the Levites, pitch their Master's tent (the tabernacle) while the others pitch theirs around it. What a joy to move when God moves and to stay when God wishes. This is to be in the center of His will—to have God in the midst of us.

One more thought just here. Was not this scene in the mind of the psalmist when he wrote, "He who dwells in the secret place of the Most High shall abide under the shadow of the Almighty" (Ps. 91:1)? No enemy, whoever he might be, could touch anyone who had been invited by a sheik into his tent. It was a place of safety. Praise God, we have been brought into His pavilion, and His banner over us is love.

2. Its Relation to Heaven. Boards on the north! Boards on the south! Boards on the west! That means the entrance is to the east; the tabernacle in the wilderness always faced east. It looked toward the sunrising. This is, or should be, the attitude of the Church. Her outlook should be eastward, toward the sunrising from whence the Lord will make His appearance: "For as the lightning comes from the east and flashes to the west, so also will the coming of the Son of Man be" (Mt. 24:27).

Remembering again that the Old Testament types are "a shadow of the good things to come, and *not the very image* of the things" (Heb. 10:1), the suggestion is not that we should have our places of worship facing east or west but that our hearts should ever be toward the coming of the Lord. Thus it is that the hope of the coming of the Lord becomes a purifying hope.

3. Position of the Furniture. Just a word about the position of the furniture. This was not left to the discretion of Moses any more than was the building. God said exactly where it should be. Just inside the gate was the brazen altar; between the altar and the tabernacle, the laver; these both were in the court. Inside the sanctuary on the south side stood the lampstand, and on the north side the table of showbread. Before the veil the altar of incense stood, and beyond the veil the ark of the covenant.

Now look at Diagram 2.* Was it chance? No! All things are given for our learning, and here we see the whole tabernacle stamped with the cross. Look at it again. The foot of the cross is in the place of suffering and death—the altar of burnt offering. The head of it is within the veil in the place of glory— the *Shekinah* of a finished work. From without to within is a straight road—via salvation, sanctification, intercession, and a torn veil into the presence of the Lord. On the right hand and on the left the arms hold out two choice blessings—fellowship at the table

*See page 34.

and unity of testimony in the golden lampstand.

4. Position While Journeying. There is one further truth on the subject of position. Our thoughts have been only on the stationary aspect. Let us look at the order of things when moving. Diagram 3* will enable us to see that order at a glance. The three tribes that were to the east of the tabernacle moved forward under the standard of Judah. Judah means "Praise of Jehovah." God always puts praise first, and the praising man always finds himself in the forefront of victory. The Gershonites removed, folded, and packed onto two wagons all the fabrics—curtains, coverings, hangings of the court, gate, and door—while the Merarite clan, which was responsible for the structural part of the building, dismantled and packed onto four wagons the boards, bars, pillars, and silver sockets of the tabernacle as well as the bronze sockets, pillars, pins, and cords of the court. These all moved next. The tribes under Reuben's standard fell in behind these wagons.

This brings us to the center of the procession, where the Kohathite clan bore their sacred charge—the furniture, including the ark covered by the veil and badgers' skins and then an outer covering of blue cloth. The covering of the various items of furniture was done by Aaron and his sons.

The table of showbread was covered with a blue cloth, upon which were then laid the dishes, pans, bowls, and pitchers for pouring—also the bread. Over all this was a scarlet cloth, then badgers' skins.

The lampstand came next: it and all its accesso-

*See page 35.

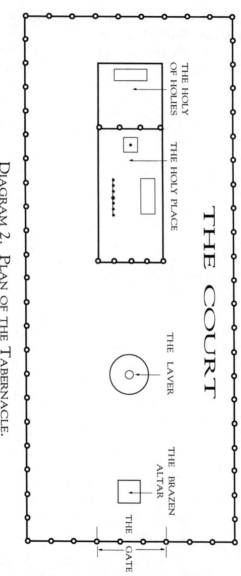

THE COURT

THE HOLY
OF HOLIES

THE HOLY PLACE

THE LAVER

THE
BRAZEN
ALTAR

THE
GATE

Diagram 2. Plan of the Tabernacle.

PILLAR OF CLOUD — (God leads the way)

JUDAH
Issachar
Zebulun
GERSHONITES
with
two wagons carrying the
CURTAINS, COVERINGS, HANGINGS, GATE, and DOOR.
MERARITES
with
four wagons carrying the
BOARDS, BARS, PILLARS, SOCKETS, COURT PILLARS,
COURT SOCKETS, PINS, and CORDS.
REUBEN
Simeon
Gad
KOHATHITES
bearing the
ARK — (God in the midst)
TABLE
LAMPSTAND
ALTAR
ALTAR
(LAVER?)
EPHRAIM
Manasseh
Benjamin
DAN
Asher
Naphtali

DIAGRAM 3. POSITION WHEN JOURNEYING.

ries were covered with a blue cloth, wrapped up in badgers' skins and put on a carrying frame. The golden altar was likewise covered with a blue cloth and badgers' skins.

The vessels of the sanctuary are next mentioned as being put into a blue cloth, covered with badgers' skins and carried on a frame or beam. These would include the many unnamed things like oil vessels.

Finally came the brazen altar. This was covered with a purple cloth upon which were placed the fire pans, meat forks, shovels, basins, etc. All was covered with badgers' skins.

No mention is made of the laver. Whether this is because it was not covered, one cannot say, but it must have been there.

It is interesting to note the variation of color and order of these coverings, all having a divine purpose.

Along with the other Kohathites was Eleazar, the son of Aaron, who was responsible for the lighting oil, the anointing oil, the incense, etc.

These holy vessels were followed by the standard of Ephraim and his confederates, while Dan, with Asher and Naphtali, came up as a rearguard. God, therefore, led the way in journeyings in the pillar of cloud, yet remained in His rightful place in their midst.

God has a task for each of us to perform, one responsibility differing from another. We must not covet another man's calling but see to it that we faithfully discharge our own. Thus will the work of the Lord make steady progress.

CHAPTER 4

General Construction

Exodus 25, 26, 27, 30, 36, 37, 38, and 40. Hebrews 9.

Then indeed, even the first covenant had ordinances of divine service and the earthly sanctuary. For a tabernacle was prepared: the first part, in which was the lampstand, the table, and the showbread, which is called the sanctuary; and behind the second veil, the part of the tabernacle which is called the Holiest of All, which had the golden altar of incense and the ark of the covenant overlaid on all sides with gold, in which were the golden pot that had the manna, Aaron's rod that budded, and the tablets of the covenant; and above it were the cherubim of glory overshadowing the mercy seat. Of these things we cannot now speak in detail.

Now when these things had been thus prepared, the priests always went into the first part of the tabernacle, performing the services. But into the second part the high priest went alone once a year, not without blood, which he offered for himself and for the people's sins committed in ignorance; the Holy Spirit indicating this, that the way into the Holiest of All was not yet made manifest while the first tabernacle was still standing. It was symbolic for the present time in which both gifts and sacrifices are offered which cannot make him who performed the service perfect in regard to the conscience—concerned only with foods and drinks, various washings, and fleshly ordinances imposed until the time of reformation.

But Christ came as High Priest of the good things to come, with the greater and more perfect tabernacle not made with hands, that is, not of this creation. Not with the blood of goats and calves, but with His own blood He entered the Most Holy Place once for all, having obtained eternal redemption. For if the blood of bulls and goats and the ashes of a heifer, sprinkling the unclean, sanctifies for the purifying of the flesh, how much more shall the blood of Christ, who through the eternal Spirit offered Himself without spot to God, purge your conscience from dead works to serve the living God?

Then likewise [Moses] sprinkled with blood both the tabernacle and all the vessels of the ministry. And according to the law almost all things are purged with blood, and without shedding of blood there is no remission. Therefore it was necessary that the copies of the things in the heavens should be purified with these, but the heavenly things themselves with better sacrifices than these. (Heb. 9:1–14, 21–23)

BEFORE taking a general survey of the whole structure, it is important to note that God began where we intend to end, at the ark of the covenant. We shall make our approach to it along the path of God's providing, from without to within. But when God laid that path it was from within to without. Notice how striking the narrative is. "And let them make Me a sanctuary, that I may dwell among them. According to all that I show you, that is, the pattern of the tabernacle and the pattern of all its furnishings, just so shall you make it. And they shall make an ark . . ." (Ex. 25:8–10). Man would erect his building first, after which he would consider the furnishings; but here, before God says one word about the building design, He describes minutely a piece of the furniture. What was the position of this ark of the covenant? It was in the Holy of Holies, or in the center of things, and everything else then adjusts itself. Is that not how God deals with man? The first great principle runs: "Is your heart right with God?" Dear reader, if your heart is not in with the divine plan, nothing else will be, and the whole teaching of the tabernacle will fail in its appeal; nor can you adjust your life to its many lessons.

Now let us take a general look at the construction of the tabernacle because, if we do not, we lose much. Many of the errors abroad today, and much of the "wrongly divided" Word, are due to failure to scan the whole horizon of divine truth before scrutinizing it minutely. We cannot discuss the full use and purpose of a stamen until we have a general idea and knowledge of flowers, botany, and bees; nor could we explain the actual results of the functioning of a carburetor and why it is in one certain place unless we have surveyed generally the whole theory of a gasoline engine. Even so with God's great truths: know the purposes of God and you will know the detail of His work. Let us see the tabernacle as a whole first—then we shall understand the component parts.

The Court. The tabernacle was positioned within a rectangular courtyard 100 cubits long and 50 cubits wide. According to Wilkinson, the cubit as found in the Nilometer of Elephantine is 20.625 inches, and as found in the wooden Egyptian cubits it is also 20.625 inches—so the courtyard was approximately 172 feet long and 86 feet wide. It was bounded by curtains, or "hangings," which were supported by sixty bronze pillars, twenty on each side and ten on each end—with two pillars united at each corner. The foundation of this court consisted of sixty sockets of bronze buried into the ground, or sand, into which the pillars were inserted. Each one of these pillars was topped off with a cap, called in the text a capital or chapiter (A.V.), which was overlaid with silver. A silver connecting bar, or fillet, held the pillars at an equal distance apart, while the curtains were attached by means of silver hooks. All was secured by cords and bronze tent pegs.

At the east end, the four center pillars formed a gate, from which hung a 20-cubit screen woven of blue, purple and scarlet yarn and fine linen thread. All other curtains of the courtyard—5 cubits high (over $8^1/_2$ feet)—were made of white linen.

The Tabernacle itself was the building standing within and toward one end of the court. It was comprised of forty-eight boards, each 10 cubits high and $1^1/_2$ cubits wide, having two tenons or feet. These were inserted into ninety-six silver sockets, each weighing approximately 125 lbs.—or 6 tons as an estimated total. The boards were united together by fifteen bars, five on each side and five on the west end. These crossbars passed through a series of rings which were joined to the boards. The east end, or front, of the building had five pillars set into sockets of bronze; these upheld a door made of curtains of blue, purple and scarlet yarn and fine linen thread. A veil of the same size and materials, embroidered with cherubim, and hanging on four pillars set into sockets of silver, made a partition between the only two rooms the tabernacle contained: the Holy Place, 20 cubits long, and the Holy of Holies, a perfect cube of 10 cubits.

One thing remains to complete the structural part, and that is the roof. This took the form of two sets of curtains and two sets of coverings. The first and innermost set consisted of ten curtains fastened together, made of blue, purple and scarlet yarn and fine linen thread with cherubim woven in. Its overall dimensions were 42 feet by 60 feet.

Over and above this were eleven curtains of goats' hair. These too were joined, and totaled 45 feet by 66 feet.

The first set of outer coverings was made of rams' skins dyed red, and the last or outer set, of badgers' skins.

It now remains to look briefly at the furniture. In the court there were two pieces made of bronze or of wood overlaid with bronze; and three pieces in the Holy Place were of gold or of wood overlaid with gold. Only one item stood in the Holy of Holies; its value was not determined by bronze or gold, but by the blood that was sprinkled on its lid, the mercy seat.

Passing through the gate of the court, we are at once confronted with the first and the largest piece of furniture—the bronze altar. Five cubits square and three cubits high, it functioned as the great place of sacrifice. Around this the people congregated, bringing their various offerings. Halfway between the altar of burnt offering and the tabernacle was the bronze laver, the place of washing for the officiating priests. We are tempted to pause and comment on these things, but we shall, in due course, deal fully with every part.

Entering now into the sacred building, we are almost startled with the amazing contrast. Everything is gold and silver, all scintillating in the flickering lights of the seven-branched lampstand (the *menorah*), a mass of beautiful ornamental work—all of it symbolical in one way or another. This stands to the left as we enter. Opposite, on the right, is the table of showbread, overlaid with gold and having upon it twelve fresh loaves of showbread. Right opposite us is the third article, with its ever-burning flame, the golden altar of incense.

Can we go beyond the veil that hangs with imposing awe and dignity behind the golden incense altar? Not then; but we can now, for the veil has been rent. If we were to have entered, what a sight would have met our eyes! There, in solitary grandeur, rested the ark of the covenant, with two beautiful cherubim and its blood-sprinkled mercy seat. Under the mercy seat were secreted the two stone tablets of testimony from Sinai, Aaron's rod that budded, and the golden pot of manna, while above the mercy seat was the glory of the *Shekinah* presence of God.

Let us come out and glance at the building again. One very conspicuous thing we have not mentioned: it is the pillar of cloud, the outward evidence of the inward presence of *Yahweh*, Jehovah God. It was the people's guide and their guard.

In the general construction one cannot help but notice that a large number of the measurements are multiples of five:

THE COURT

60	pillars	12 x 5
60	capitals	12 x 5
60	sockets.	12 x 5
120	pins	24 x 5
100	cubits long	20 x 5
50	cubits wide	10 x 5
5	cubits high	1 x 5

THE ENTRANCES

Gate ... 20 cubits wide	4 x 5
Gate ..... 5 cubits high	1 x 5
Door ... 10 cubits wide	2 x 5
Door ... 10 cubits high	2 x 5
Door .... on 5 pillars	1 x 5
Veil .... 10 cubits wide	2 x 5
Veil .... 10 cubits high	2 x 5

THE TABERNACLE

30	cubits long	6 x 5
10	cubits wide	2 x 5
10	cubits high	2 x 5
100	silver sockets	20 x 5
15	bars	3 x 5
5	bars each side	1 x 5
10	curtains	2 x 5
50	clasps	10 x 5
100	blue loops	20 x 5

HOLY OF HOLIES

10 x 10 x 10 cubits	2 x 5

BRONZE ALTAR

5 x 5 cubits	1 x 5
5 vessels	1 x 5
5 animals	1 x 5
5 offerings	1 x 5

IN THE ARK

10 commandments	2 x 5

HOLY PLACE

20 cubits long ...	4 x 5
10 cubits wide ...	2 x 5
10 cubits high ...	2 x 5

What does this all mean? Five is the number of grace, as seen in such instances as the feeding of 5,000 people with five barley loaves, a wonderful act of grace on the part of the Lord; and when David took five stones from the brook he revealed that he was depending on the "unmerited favor" (grace) of the Lord God. In the Church of God it is grace everywhere, "all of grace," abounding grace—and blue, the "heavenly" color, is found everywhere in the tabernacle, covering the furniture, and on the garments of the high priest.

Concerning the value of the tabernacle, it has been estimated from Exodus 38:24–31, in the following terms:

	TALENTS	SHEKELS	
Gold	29	730	$877,300
Silver	100	1,775	195,136
Bronze	70	2,400	690

$1,073,126

Adding to this the cost of wood, fabrics, priestly garments, precious stones for the breastplate, etc., one and a quarter million dollars [1963 dollars, that is] would be a reasonable estimate, without labor.

Chapter 5

Silver Sockets

Exodus 30:11–16. Exodus 38:25–28.
Matthew 17:24–27. 1 Peter 1:18–19.

Then the Lord spoke to Moses, saying: "When you take the census of the children of Israel for their number, then every man shall give a ransom for himself to the Lord, when you number them, that there may be no plague among them when you number them. This is what everyone among those who are numbered shall give: half a shekel according to the shekel of the sanctuary (a shekel is twenty gerahs). The half-shekel shall be an offering to the Lord. Everyone included among those who are numbered, from twenty years old and above, shall give an offering to the Lord. The rich shall not give more and the poor shall not give less than half a shekel, when you give an offering to the Lord, to make atonement for yourselves. And you shall take the atonement money of the children of Israel, and shall appoint it for the service of the tabernacle of meeting, that it may be a memorial for the children of Israel before the Lord, to make atonement for yourselves." (Ex. 30:11–16)

And the silver from those who were numbered of the congregation was one hundred talents and one thousand seven hundred and seventy-five shekels, according to the shekel of the sanctuary: a bekah for each man (that is,

half a shekel, according to the shekel of the sanctuary),
for everyone included in the numbering from twenty years
old and above, for six hundred and three thousand, five
hundred and fifty men. And from the hundred talents of
silver were cast the sockets of the sanctuary and the bases
of the veil: one hundred sockets from the hundred talents, one talent for each socket. Then from the one thousand seven hundred and seventy-five shekels he made
hooks for the pillars, overlaid their capitals, and made
bands for them. (Ex. 38:25–28)

REFERENCE has already been made to the fact
that all the materials for construction of the
tabernacle came by freewill offering from a willing
people. There was one exception, which we will deal
with here.

God instructed that when the men twenty years
of age and upwards were numbered for the army,
they should pay an amount in silver as a ransom for
their lives. This appears to be a strange action, especially so when we see the reason: "that there be no
plague among them" (Ex. 30:12). If they had paid a
levy or tax, one might have passed it over. But no, it
is called a ransom. Why? And why should numbering cause a plague? God had not forbidden the numbering of Israel at this time—or at any rate, no pro-
hibition is recorded. I suspect it was that He knew
the heart of man was full of pride—a pride that tends
to depend on numbers rather than on God, a pride
that often "goes before a fall." And so He demanded
from each one, at the time of their census, a piece of
silver. It was called a "ransom," and as such it reminded the man being enlisted into the army of Is-

rael—which was the army of God—that he himself was unworthy of such a calling. It is also called "atonement money," "atonement" meaning "to cover." His sin, therefore, was covered before he committed it. In other words, it was God's merciful provision against the sins of His people.

But surely there is no covering for sin apart from shed blood, is there? That is so—but the Lord is laying a foundation with regard to type, and silver is the price of life. Men were bought and sold for silver. We remember Joseph who was sold for twenty pieces of silver, and the Lord Jesus Christ whose life was betrayed for thirty pieces of silver. Similarly it was in the payment of half a shekel that the men of Israel were delivered from the visitation of a plague. So silver typifies "redemption."

It is well to point out here the difference between "atonement" and "redemption," because Christ is often referred to as atoning for sin. He never did. Only once does the word occur in the New Testament, i.e., Romans 5:11b: "By whom we have now received the atonement"(A.V.). The Greek word is *katallage* and is translated everywhere else as "reconciliation" or "reconciling" (and the NKJV has corrected it here). To "atone" means to "cover." That is what laws and offerings did, but they did not *erase* sin. "For what the law could not do in that it was weak through the flesh, God did by sending His own Son in the likeness of sinful flesh, on account of sin: He condemned sin in the flesh" (Rom. 8:3). Christ's work was to redeem, or to set us free from the power of sin and death.

"Half a shekel, according to the shekel of the sanctuary," was what each man paid. It weighed a quarter of an ounce and was equal to thirty-one cents [in 1963]. "The rich shall not give more and the poor shall not give less": each man was to pay for himself. God fixed the price and man must comply. There was no question of personal opinion. How like salvation! God has laid down His conditions. It is faith in Christ, whether we be high or low, rich or poor, learned or ignorant, prince or pauper, black or white, young or old. The condition is simple and within the reach of all—faith in Christ.

When these men were numbered, the total was 603,550 (Num. 1:45–46). Each paying his ransom money, this brought in a good revenue, totaling 301,775 shekels of silver. The Lord had specified how the accumulated silver was to be utilized. It was "for the service of the tabernacle"—primarily, at this first census, for the making of the silver sockets that became the foundation of the tabernacle. Three thousand shekels equaled a talent, so there were a hundred sockets each weighing a talent of 125 lbs. apiece. Ninety-six of these were to make foundations for the boards, and the other four served as sockets for the pillars of the veil. This foundation of more than six tons of silver was necessary because of Israel's being in the wilderness—a sandy region. The Lord Jesus said that a man who built his house on sand is foolish. Sand is unstable. Are not the ideas, theories, and doctrines of men always changing? They cannot be relied upon, and so we need a foundation for our faith that is solid, dependable, and lasting. That basis is found in the redemption that is in Christ Jesus and His death.

The foundation of the congregation in the wilderness, then, was the price of ransom; similarly, the Church of the New Testament is resting entirely on Christ's redemptive work.

There remained 1,775 shekels, part of which were used to form silver fillets or connecting bars and hooks; some also were used for the overlaying of the capitals. Further reference will be made to these in the chapter on the court.

May not the Apostle Peter have had the tabernacle in mind when he wrote his first epistle, for from it he seems to have drawn out a spiritual application when he said, "Knowing that you were not redeemed with corruptible things, like silver and gold, from your aimless conduct received by tradition from your fathers, but with the precious blood of Christ, as of a lamb without blemish and without spot" (1 Pet. 1:18–19)?

There is a very interesting connection between the New Testament and the Old with regard to this ransom money. It is to be found in Matthew 17:24–27: "And when they had come to Capernaum, those who received the temple tax came to Peter and said, 'Does your Teacher not pay the temple tax?' He said, 'Yes.' And when he had come into the house, Jesus anticipated him, saying, 'What do you think, Simon? From whom do the kings of the earth take customs or taxes, from their own sons or from strangers?' Peter said to Him, 'From strangers.' Jesus said to him, 'Then the sons are free. Nevertheless, lest we offend them, go to the sea, cast in a hook, and take the fish that comes up first. And when you have opened its mouth, you will find a piece of money; that take and give it to them for Me and you.'"

The tax here referred to was not a national tax imposed by a ruler. That was demanded without question. This tax was a custom that came into vogue as a result of the ransom money paid in Exodus 30. In acknowledgment of God's goodness, all men twenty years of age and upwards paid annually, by their own free will, a half-shekel of the sanctuary as a contribution towards the maintenance of the temple. It was, therefore, a kind of church tax. The collectors of this money came on this occasion to Peter asking (not demanding), "Does your Teacher not pay the temple tax?" Peter, in his impetuous manner, seems to answer without any thought or consideration, "Yes," and then enters the house evidently to appeal to the Lord. But Jesus was the first to speak. "What do you think, Simon? From whom do the kings of the earth collect customs and taxes? From their own sons, or from others?" Peter was caught. The truth was manifest. Peter had answered wrongly. The members of a royal family were always exempt from paying taxes. Jesus draws a comparison between Himself, the King of kings, and an earthly king. He had claimed that He was the Son of God. If this tax was for the upkeep of God's house, then God's Son was exempt—"Then the sons are free." Then in the Lord's usual gracious way—as Peter had said "Yes," and as the people might misconstrue Christ's action—He, not willing to cause offence, said to Peter, "Go to the sea and throw out your line. Take the first fish you catch; open its mouth and you will find a coin." The fact that the fish had a coin in its mouth was not the miracle. The Rev. L.T. Pearson points out in his book *Through the Holy Land* that, among the many species of fish found in the Sea of Galilee is one called the *musht,* commonly known now as "Peter's fish." "The male," says Mr. Pearson, "has a habit of carrying the young in its mouth, and of sucking them in in time of danger. Sometimes it will carry a stone or other obstacle to keep the young out. The *musht* has been found to have objects other than stones in its mouth. They are attracted by bright objects, and even coins have been picked up by them."

Wherein lies the miracle then? First, the Lord said, "Take up the *first* fish." Seeing that there are some forty or more species of fish in the Sea of Galilee, it could have been any other of these; and second, "when you have opened its mouth, you will find a piece of money." The footnote in the 1611 A.V. edition says, "A stater. It is half an ounce of silver"—now about sixty-four cents in value. That is double the amount paid by the men of Israel in Exodus 38:26. "And give it to them for Me and you." The Lord paid for Peter as well as for Himself. Since that time He has paid the price of redemption for all men by the giving of Himself and the shedding of His blood. Oh, glorious foundation of the Church of Christ!

CHAPTER 6

The Boards and Bars

Exodus 26:15–29. Exodus 36:20–34.

"And for the tabernacle you shall make the boards of acacia wood, standing upright. Ten cubits shall be the length of a board, and a cubit and a half shall be the width of each board. Two tenons shall be in each board for binding one to another. Thus you shall make for all the boards of the tabernacle. And you shall make the boards for the tabernacle, twenty boards for the south side. You shall make forty sockets of silver under the twenty boards: two sockets under one board for its two tenons, and two sockets under another board for its two tenons. And for the second side of the tabernacle, the north side, there shall be twenty boards and their forty sockets of silver: two sockets under one board, and two sockets under another board. For the far side of the tabernacle, westward, you shall make six boards. And you shall also make two boards for the two back corners of the tabernacle. They shall be coupled together at the bottom and they shall be coupled together at the top by one ring. Thus it shall be for both of them. They shall be for the two corners. So there shall be eight boards with their sockets of silver—sixteen sockets—two sockets under one board, and two sockets under another board.

"And you shall make bars of acacia wood: five for the

boards on one side of the tabernacle, five bars for the boards on the other side of the tabernacle, and five bars for the boards of the side of the tabernacle, for the far side westward. The middle bar shall pass through the midst of the boards from end to end. You shall overlay the boards with gold, make their rings of gold as holders for the bars, and overlay the bars with gold." (Ex. 26:15–29)

"AND for the tabernacle you shall make the boards of acacia wood, standing upright." The last two words of that statement are rather impressive—"standing upright." Are you, Christian reader, standing upright? Many are sitting at ease, others are reclining in indolence—but let us consider the matter.

In the previous chapter we dealt with the silver sockets as a type of the redemptive work of the Lord Jesus Christ, by whose blood the foundation of the true Church has been laid. These boards, standing on such a foundation and forming the dwelling place of God, must naturally turn our thoughts to the believers, the living stones of God's temple, who rest upon the finished work of Jesus' cross.

Let us look first at the characteristics revealed in the boards.

1. They Were Made of Acacia Wood. The acacia tree, from whence such wood comes, is a native of the Sinai Peninsula and the desert. There was a time when we, who are now the saints of God, were strangers to His grace. We grew in the world and drew from the world's barrenness that which met the needs of our life. In such a condition we were never truly happy nor satisfied.

2. These Trees Were Cut Down. Saul of Tarsus was one of these trees. While on his way to Damascus, he was met by God and was cut down to the earth. Do not we remember when the Spirit of God cut across our lives and laid us low, causing us to say, "Lord, what do you want me to do?" This means a severance from the old life—our link with the earth broken.

3. The Trees Were Then Cut Up. This was a very necessary thing because the natural condition of the acacia tree is knots and twists. There is nothing straight about it, and it is, therefore, of little or no use for building purposes unless trimmed. What an outstanding type of the believer! How we do need to be straightened, and oh, how we object sometimes! The work of the Spirit is a continuous one. So many feel they have all when they receive salvation, but that is far from true. There is development, a shaping into Christlike character, a daily growing in grace and in knowledge of Christ Jesus the Lord. The sap of selfishness must be dried out; the knots of hardness must be smoothed down to gentleness and compassion; and the twists of halfheartedness must be straightened—for they will never allow for perfect fitting and a unity in the Spirit, the state in which the Lord always delights to dwell.

The acacia boards, having thus been prepared so far as their natural condition was concerned, were then overlaid, and thus beautified, with pure gold. How suggestive—remembering that wood is a type of humanity and gold of divinity, because of its imperishableness. God not only works in the natural man and transforms the human nature, but He also clothes us with His own divine nature. Peter tells us that we become "partakers of the divine nature" (2 Pet. 1:4).

So much for the nature of the boards; now a word as to their shape. Each of the forty-eight boards was ten cubits long (17 feet) and a cubit and a half wide (2 1/2 feet). The thickness is not stated. On the face of each board there were rings through which bars were passed. Each board had at its lower extremity two tenons—projections that allowed it to stand solidly in the sockets of its foundation. The mention of two tenons carries our thoughts back to the verse quoted at the head of this chapter, "And for the tabernacle you shall make the boards of acacia wood, *standing upright.*" All ordinary tents were erected by *driving in* stakes and pins; their existence was dependent on a grip of the desert. But to these boards of God's tent were given two "feet," and for them were provided two sockets, so that they stood *independent* of the sand of the desert. They stood upright *in* the desert and not *of* it. Once, as trees, they were well rooted in it. What separated the boards from the sand? Silver—a ransom price. You, dear reader, if ransomed by Christ, are not your own. You, too, should be *in* the world but not *of* it, separated because of the blood of Christ. "Come out from among them and be separate, says the Lord. Do not touch what is unclean . . ." (2 Cor. 6:17). Are you among those who say, "It is difficult to stand"? May we remind you that God has given you two feet and two silver sockets. There are so many Christians who have one foot established in "the redemption that is in Christ Jesus" but have their other foot in something else—pleasure, perhaps, or politics, or social standing; or maybe there is an interest in one of the various "isms" of the day. We would not condemn some of these things if they were in their rightful place, but when they are put on a par with Christian living, so as to cause one's testimony and faith to be weakened, then stability is lost.

While these boards have no relation to the desert, they certainly have one with each other and with God. First note their union with each other. Forty-eight boards, 10 x 1¹/₂ cubits, stood so "fitly framed together" as to become one building. They all stood, as it were, shoulder to shoulder with such a unity that daylight could not be seen between them. There was no rubbing or chafing because they were so well-balanced. All this was the result of being on a solid foundation. It is when believers are out fundamentally that they are out with each other. One person leaning toward this theory and another toward that dogma means a loss of unity and fellowship into which the Enemy of souls enters and splits the work, or else he causes a chafing that creates an irritability which brings discord and discontent. Not only were the boards "joined together by what every joint supplies" (Eph. 4:16) but they were equal in their height, forty-eight boards ten cubits high. How practical is the teaching of the tabernacle! Solomon said that "jealousy is cruel as the grave" (Song 8:6). It has ruined many a man, but God would have us learn from the evenness of height that there is no room nor place in the church for one to look down on or despise another, or to be jealous of another. We must follow the inspired exhortation of the Apostle Paul who said, "Let each esteem others better than himself" (Phil. 2:3b). Let us aspire to become "a perfect man, to the measure of the stature of the fullness of Christ" (Eph. 4:13b).

Second, their relationship to God must be considered. "Twenty boards for the south side . . . twenty boards for the north side . . . and eight boards for the west side" means that the tabernacle always faced eastward—that is, toward the sunrising. The suggestion is that this building always looked toward God. In any case, this should certainly be the attitude of the Church of the present day. We should, as we pass through this night of sorrow, keep our eyes toward daybreak—the east—for when the Sun of Righteousness shall appear, shadows will flee away:

"Turn your eyes upon Jesus,
   Look full in His wonderful face,
   And the things of earth will grow strangely dim
   In the light of His glory and grace."

The two corner boards have caused much perplexity as to how they were fastened together. The writer, having built several models of the tabernacle, has considered this problem—as well as that of the unstated board thickness. From the practical standpoint, it is to be noted that nothing is said of the complete measurement of the tabernacle's length, namely: thirty cubits. Commentators and others have calculated it from twenty boards, each a cubit-and-a-half broad. If this were the complete length, however, then one could not fit inside it a Holy of Holies 10 x 10 cubits and a Holy Place 20 x 10 cubits (these measurements must be on the inside—one never measures rooms from the outside), because there must be a deduction for the thickness of the back boards, together with the thickness of the pillars of the veil and those that support the front door. The outer measurement must, therefore, be greater, and the text allows for it in the two corner boards. In the Hebrew here the word "corner" is *mequtsoah*, meaning "angle." Now take a board, cut it lengthwise down the center in a miter box, reverse one piece and join the two pieces together again, and you have a "corner" or "angle" board for each of the two corners.

In this circumstance the corner boards would add two half-cubits to the six other boards, making the required ten cubits for the width; also it would increase the total length by half a cubit. This would allow the pillars of the veil to be half a cubit in diameter. The thickness of the boards, back and sides, would be adjusted in the miter cut. The rooms will then be found fitting according to the prescribed measurements. The top and bottom of these corner boards fitted into a girdle. Thus the whole was strengthened and locked. Has not the Word of God told us that Jesus Christ is the chief cornerstone, the source of strength and stability for all believers?

Into each board were put, presumably, three rings through which the bars were to pass. Some have suggested that the three rings are a picturing of the triune blessing: the grace of the Lord Jesus, the love of God, and the fellowship of the Holy Spirit. Others say that they represent faith, hope, and love; and still others suggest that they point to the work of the Triune God on behalf of each believer. All these thoughts are good, but the writer prefers the last, because it is so encouraging to be reminded that Father, Son, and Spirit are working for and on our behalf. We can find the three statements all in one chapter—Romans 8: "What then shall we say to these things? *If God is for us*, who can be against us?" (v. 31). "Who is he who condemns? It is *Christ* who died, and furthermore is also risen, who is even at the right hand of God, who also makes intercession *for us*" (v. 34). "Likewise the Spirit also helps in our weaknesses. For we do not know what we should pray for as we ought, but the *Spirit* Himself makes intercession *for us* with groanings which cannot be uttered" (v. 26).

Silver sockets kept the boards from sinking into the sand or losing equality of height. Their close relationship with each other prevented a tilting to the right or left. One thing remained: they could lean backwards or forwards and so get out of line and touch with each other, except for a yet further provision made by the Lord. "You shall make bars for the boards and overlay them with pure gold." These bars consolidated the whole into one. There were five bars on each of the sides: north, south, and west. The center bar went from end to end and the other four were apparently half lengths, two above and two below the center one. There are many who teach us that the center bar was invisible and was designed to go through the inside of the boards. Let us spend a few moments considering this, as its position makes a difference to our interpretation.

Was it logically and mechanically possible? If it was possible, it is most improbable. Each board was approximately 17 feet high and $2^1/2$ feet wide. What was the thickness? We are not told. Twenty boards of this width stood side by side, therefore the bar that shot through from end to end was nearly fifty-two feet long. What thickness would that bar have to be not to snap? Having estimated your measurements, could you get your bar through the inside of your boards; and having put it in, could you withdraw it? Remember, the bar was neither metal nor bamboo, but acacia wood overlaid with gold. I cannot imagine that your measurements, whatever you have estimated them to be, will allow for this—and even if they do, were you to bore a large enough hole right through the center of such a board, you would have robbed it of its strength. A wind, or even the weight of the expanse of curtains and coverings, would snap the board completely in two. Furthermore, those who give expression to an "invisible bar" in typifying the subject refer to the bars as representing the Trinity of the Godhead—Father, Son, and Holy Spirit—stating that the center bar speaks of the Holy Spirit because He is invisible. Two errors are obvious in this method of interpretation. First, only three bars are referred to, while Scripture speaks of five; and second, surely God the Father and God the Son are as invisible to the human eye as is God the Holy Spirit!

Enough for the negative side; let us now think on the positive side. (1) You shall "make rings as holders for the bars," not for some of the bars. (2) "The middle bar shall pass through the midst of the boards." 8 ft. 6 in. from the top and 8 ft. 6 in. from the bottom is surely in the midst of the boards. The difficult statement of Exodus 36:33 can be harmonized with this because, while it says "pass through," it does not say "inside."

An illustration will help just here. A car skids on the road and passes through a crowd of people who are standing on the corner. Does that car go through the inside of each individual? Of course not! The illustration is self-explanatory.

Now that we see five bars all passing similarly through rings around the outside of the boards, binding them together into one complete structure, we come to the more important thing. What do they teach us? The Apostle Paul tells us that God has given five gifts of ministry to the Church; they are found in Ephesians 4:11: "And He Himself gave some to be apostles, some prophets, some evangelists, and some pastors and teachers." These bars and ministries are readily harmonized. The first two ministries are represented by the two lower bars—". . . built on the foundation of the apostles and prophets . . ." (Eph. 2:20). This, of course, does not mean that Peter, Paul, and others are the foundation of our faith. The foundation is lower than the bars and is definitely Christ's redemptive work. It means that apostles and prophets were the substructure of ministry while ours is part of the superstructure. The center bar, reaching from end to end, would remind us of the center ministry stated—that of the evangelist. What an extensive work is his; how far-reaching! "Go into all the world and preach the gospel to *every creature*" (Mark 16:15). The evangelist having done his part, then come the labors of the pastor and teacher: one to shepherd and care for the flock, the other to instruct them in divine things and so ever seek to lift them higher and higher. These two ministries are typified by the two top bars.

To say that these bars thus speak of church ministry is no speculation, for if we read on in Ephesians 4, "comparing spiritual things with spiritual," we shall find that both the bars and the gifts were given for a similar purpose, "for the equipping of the saints for the work of ministry, for the edifying of the body of Christ, till we all come to the unity of the faith and of the knowledge of the Son of God, to a perfect man, to the measure of the stature of the fullness of Christ; that we should no longer be children, tossed to and fro and carried about with every wind of doctrine, by the trickery of men, in the cunning craftiness by which they lie in wait to deceive, but, speaking the truth in love, may grow up in all things into Him who is the head—Christ—from whom the whole body, joined and knit together by what every joint supplies, according to the effective working by which every part does its share, causes growth of the body for the edifying of itself in love" (Eph. 4:12–16).

Taking away the bars from the boards would mean

that a broadside wind would scatter the boards like ninepins, and the whole structure would collapse. Likewise if we had not this God-given ministry in the Church, every wind of doctrine would scatter the flock; but God has not only established the Church in the present dispensation, He has also supplied the means of consolidation. Therefore, "touch not the Lord's anointed" and despise not the ministry.

Still writing to the Ephesians, the apostle draws yet another comparison between the tabernacle of the Old Testament and the Church of the New Testament. "In whom the whole building, being joined together, grows into a holy temple in the Lord, in whom you also are being built together for a habitation of God in the Spirit" (Eph. 2:21–22).

The tabernacle was a habitation of God in wood and gold. The Church is a habitation of God in spiritual and living stones.

· CHAPTER 7 ·

The Curtains and Coverings

Exodus 26:1–14. Exodus 36:8–19.

"Moreover you shall make the tabernacle with ten curtains woven of fine linen thread, and blue and purple and scarlet yarn; with artistic designs of cherubim you shall weave them. The length of each curtain shall be twenty-eight cubits, and the width of each curtain four cubits. And every one of the curtains shall have the same measurements. Five curtains shall be coupled to one another, and the other five curtains shall be coupled to one another. And you shall make loops of blue yarn on the edge of the curtain on the selvedge of one set, and likewise you shall do on the outer edge of the other curtain of the second set. Fifty loops you shall make in the one curtain, and fifty loops you shall make on the edge of the curtain that is on the end of the second set, that the loops may be clasped to one another. And you shall make fifty clasps of gold, and couple the curtains together with the clasps, so that it may be one tabernacle.

"You shall also make curtains of goats' hair, to be a tent over the tabernacle. You shall make eleven curtains. The length of each curtain shall be thirty cubits, and the width of each curtain four cubits; and the eleven curtains shall all have the same measurements. And you shall couple five curtains by themselves and six curtains by themselves, and you shall double over the sixth curtain at the forefront of the tent. You shall make fifty loops on the edge of the curtain that is outermost in one set, and fifty loops on the edge of the curtain of the second set. And you shall make fifty bronze clasps, put the clasps into the loops, and couple the tent together, that it may be one. The remnant that remains of the curtains of the tent, the half curtain that remains, shall hang over the back of the tabernacle. And a cubit on one side and a cubit on the other side, of what remains of the length of the curtains of the tent, shall hang over the sides of the tabernacle, on this side and on that side, to cover it.

"You shall also make a covering of rams' skins dyed red for the tent, and a covering of badger skins above that." (Exodus 26:1–14)

THE CURTAINS and the coverings—in other words, the roof of the tabernacle—will complete the structure except for the pillars of the door and of the veil. There are two sets of curtains and two sets of coverings. We will not deal with these in the same order in which they are recorded in Exodus 26, from inside to outside, because that is God's order. He plans from within the sanctuary—we approach from without.

In each instance we shall observe that they teach us something about the Christ. So we see Him as the "foundation," "chief cornerstone" and "top stone" of the Church—or Christ as our all, and in all.

First Covering—Badgers' Skins. One verse is all that we have that mentions the two outer coverings: badgers' skins and rams' skins. As to whether the animal referred to as a "badger" in our translation belonged to the land or the sea is difficult to ascertain; the latter appears more likely. In fact, translations differ widely: some say "porpoise skins," some "dolphin skins," some "sea cow [i.e., dugong] hide." At any rate, the badger that we in the West know was an unknown animal on the Sinai Peninsula. The only other reference to this animal in Scripture is in Ezekiel 16:10, where we read: "I . . . gave you sandals of badger skin." We conclude, therefore, that these were skins of a preservative nature, used to protect what was beneath from exposure to storm, rain, sand, and scorching sun. It undoubtedly was a weather-beaten skin with no beauty or attractiveness. This outer skin would be practically all that could be seen by any onlooker, and it formed a roof or tent over the tabernacle.

Here, then, is our first picture of Christ. He has become the covering of all those who put their trust in Him. The wrath which was our due fell on Him; the storm cloud of judgment broke upon His head; the scorching sun of infernal hatred spent its rays upon His body. "He is despised and rejected by men, a man of sorrows and acquainted with grief," until it was said of Him, "[He is] as a root out of dry ground. He has no form or comeliness; and when we see Him, there is no beauty that we should desire Him." What does the world see in Jesus today? Nothing. Why? Because it does not know Him. But we do—because we were not content to look on such a marred form without seeking to find out the reason for such suffering. Our eyes, by grace, have pierced the badger skin of the human frame and beheld the rams' skins, which have shown us both the reason and the motive.

Second Covering—Rams' Skins Dyed Red. The ram is the animal of substitution. It takes the place of another, as seen in the story of Abraham and Isaac and in several of the Levitical offerings. It is also the animal used for the consecration of the priesthood, and is spoken of as the "ram of the consecration" in Exodus 29 and Leviticus 8. Cannot we link these two truths together in Christ as we see Him consecrating Himself to the work of the cross that He might become our substitute? I should have died, but He died *for* me, as the ram did for Isaac. Skins (we are not told of what animal) were used in the garden of Eden as a substitute for the fig leaves of man's providing.

We proceed a little deeper toward the interior and meet with the two sets of fabric curtains that roofed over the framework. It is very important to note that the outer set of curtains was always called the *ohel* or "tent," and the inner the *mishkan* or "tabernacle." Strictly speaking, the tabernacle was not the tent, and the tent was not the tabernacle. The tabernacle was inside the tent and the tent covered the tabernacle. The tabernacle was God's dwelling place. The tent was man's meeting place.

First Curtain—Goats' Hair. It was actually a set of eleven curtains, each thirty cubits long and four cubits wide. Joined together, they formed one great canopy, thirty cubits by forty-four cubits, covering the tabernacle in its entirety.

Of what were these curtains made? Goats' hair.

What was their color? Black. It is here that many people make a big mistake. They usually describe these curtains, whether by picture or word, as *white* and as representing the righteousness of Christ. They conclude this because goats' hair is normally white in our Western world. But the tabernacle was built in an area of the world where a white goat is a rarity: Middle Eastern goats are black. This, of course, completely reverses the spiritual application propounded by many.

Before proceeding further, let us consider two references in Scripture which substantiate the fact that goats' hair is black. Bear in mind that all tents in the Middle East are made of goats' hair and are spoken of by the Bedouin as their "home of hair." Now turn to the Song of Solomon 1:5: "I am *black*, but lovely, O daughters of Jerusalem, like the *tents* of Kedar, like the curtains of Solomon." In addition, read carefully the story of Jacob and Laban. Both were cunning and crafty men; both were always out for personal advantage; both sought to outwit the other when the opportunity afforded itself. These two schemers are found bargaining in Genesis 30:25–43. Jacob proposes to Laban that he should have all the streaked, speckled, and spotted goats. In other words, all that were other than black would become Jacob's. If, in the natural course of events, these were in the majority, we ought not imagine that a man of Laban's wily character would agree. But in verse 34, Laban says, "Oh, that it were according to your word." This surely is sufficient evidence that the goats were normally black. Then it was that Jacob began his plan to get the better of his uncle: by putting whitened sticks before the watering troughs of the goats that were copulating, he mesmerized them—or so he thought—causing them to bring forth kids with unusual characteristics: they were born streaked, speckled, and spotted. And so he got the best of the bargain.

Remembering what has already been remarked about the difference between the *ohel* and the *mishkan*, we see that God in the tabernacle revealed that He would dwell within the "house of hair" even as *Israel* dwelt in tents. What a foreview of *Immanuel*—"God with us," or God in Christ Jesus dwelling in the same human form in which we find ourselves. It has been said that a Middle Eastern shepherd wears a sheepskin coat because he believes the sheep like to see him as one of them. The idea may be sentimental, but the ideal is seen in Jesus, "For verily he took not on him the nature of angels; but he took on him the seed of Abraham. Wherefore in all things it behoved him to be made like unto his brethren, that he might be a merciful and faithful high priest in things pertaining to God . . ." (Heb. 2:16–17, A.V.).

A word further concerning the color of these curtains. As has already been intimated, their color being black instead of white, we must necessarily change the usual interpretation. Instead of the suggested righteousness, we see Christ as the sin offering. We shall note that this interpretation produces a beautiful harmony with the general teaching of Scripture concerning the goat, for the goat is a type of sin:

A kid of the goats was the animal for a sin offering (Lev. 9:3).

Two goats were used on the day of atonement (Lev. 16:5–28).

Sheep and goats represent saved and unsaved people (Matt. 25:32).

Christ came in the likeness of sinful flesh (Rom. 8:3).

Also, we use black as the emblematic color of sin.

Furthermore, this interpretation is in harmony with the general teaching about the curtains and coverings, for all three outer fabrics speak of Christ's suffering: badgers' skins, the despised One; rams' skins, the substitute through death; goats' hair, the sin offering. These all bring us to the inner beauty seen in the fourth curtain and in Christ's perfect life; and thus it was that He brought "many sons to glory."

But first, a word concerning the number of goats' hair curtains used. There were eleven of them, sewn together in groups of five and six, and then the two pieces were united by fifty bronze clasps ("taches"— A.V.) that attached one hundred loops, fifty loops being in each of the two selvedges. (We shall say more about these clasps later, as there are others for the next set of curtains.) Eleven, we are told, is the number of disorganization. Two illustrations of this number will explain:

1. When Joseph told his dream of eleven stars doing obeisance to him, he offended his brothers who, as a result, sold the dreamer and so

brought disorganization to the family (Gen. 37).
2. The betrayal of Christ by Judas resulted in his
   leaving the twelve, and from the Passover Feast
   to Pentecost it was always the "eleven." During this period everything was disorganized so
   far as the disciples were concerned.

Christ, as the sin offering, certainly disorganized the
work of the Enemy and put him to flight.

Ten curtains, we find, just covered the tabernacle;
the eleventh—or the sixth as it is called in verse
nine (showing the order of their placement)—was
to be doubled over at the forefront of the tent. When
the outer coverings were put into position, they con-
cealed all the curtains except this one thus hanging—so Israel saw only one-eleventh of the goats'
hair curtain while the ten-elevenths remained un-
seen by man. Looking into the life of Christ, we
very soon see the meaning of it all. Christ spent
approximately thirty-three years on this earth: that
is, eleven threes. Ten elevenths of His life, which is
thirty years, were spent in secret except for the incident at the age of twelve when He, as a Jewish boy,
arrived at His coming-of-age and so was brought to
the temple. Then, when Jesus had reached the age
of thirty, John said, "Behold," and pointed the people
to "the Lamb of God, who takes away the sin of the
world." And so, for the last eleventh of His life, in a
three-year ministry, He was revealed to the world.
Revealed as what?—the sin offering, as John declared
Him to be. No wonder the Emmaus disciples said
their hearts burned within them as He taught them

from Moses and the Prophets! Surely these things cause our hearts also to burn and our souls to rejoice.

Now let us see what we can learn as we take yet another step and examine the . . .

Second Curtain—Fine Linen Cloth. This set of innermost curtains is always called the *mishkan*, meaning "residence," and is usually translated "the tabernacle"—being called such because it served as the ceiling, without which the building was not a true house. It consisted of ten curtains, each twenty-eight cubits by four cubits. These long panels, handwoven on looms about seven feet wide, were then sewn together at their edges into two sets of five. Loops of blue material were made along the selvedge of the end curtains of each set—fifty along each. Fifty gold clasps were used to fasten the curtains together as a unit. The total dimension was twenty-eight cubits by forty cubits (48 feet by 68 3/4 feet).

These curtains were woven of finely twisted linen thread and blue, purple and scarlet yarn, and had a design of cherubim worked into them. (Have you noticed that the colors are always mentioned in the same order?) Blue, purple and scarlet—purple is the harmonizing color that brings the other two together. Much can be said concerning these three colors and their significance, but we shall content ourselves with a bare outline here and will touch upon the subject again. (These colors are to be seen also in the fabric at the gate, the door, the veil, and in the high priest's ephod.)

Blue. This is a heavenly color, and is always asso-

ciated with the blue sky. It is the emblematic color
of divinity and grace. We will think only of the divinity aspect now. Look up into the beautiful blue-
vaulted heavens—how impressive, how serene!
Sometimes clouds come between and temporarily blot
out the sky, but they never pollute it. It is high above
all the clouds, mists, and fogs. Nothing can pierce
the heavens, nor even reach them. What is man's
journey to the moon when we remember that it is
only 238,000 miles from the earth, while the sun is
93,000,000 miles away. Also light, traveling at
186,000 miles per second, takes four years to come
from the nearest star. Likewise, boundless is the divinity of Christ.

Man gets into his "higher-critical balloon" and
propounds some modern concept of God and Christ,
but how foolish. Christ is divine; who can approach
such a subject? Let men obscure the view with their
clouds of doubt and their mists of modernism—what
of it? The clouds will disperse, "moderns" will disap-
pear, but He remains. Remember, dear reader, even
when, because of clouds, you cannot see Him, He
remains. The heavens are illimitable, unchangeable,
and eternal. So is Christ in His great uncreated glory
and unfathomable divinity. One holds the pen of a
ready writer when writing concerning *Him*. Enough
to say that blue in these curtains typifies Jesus as the
divine Son of God.

Scarlet. We bring the third color under observation next—rather contrary to scriptural order, but
for reasons readily seen when we deal with the purple.
If we were in Palestine, "the land of the Book," we

would appreciate the significance of this color more because, in many places, it is the color of the Palestinian earth. So, turning from blue to bright red, we drop our eyes from heaven to earth. "Adam," the name given to man in Genesis, comes from the root word meaning "red earth." Adam, the first man, was of the earth—made from dust of the ground. Jesus was the second Man, the Lord from heaven.

Another beautiful illustration of this truth is to be found in Genesis 25:25: "And the first [twin] came out red. He was like an hairy garment all over; so they called his name Esau." Esau, then, was a red-haired man; he was also an earthly man in his desires, and to satisfy an earthly gratification he sold his birthright—a spiritual heritage went for a meal of red stew. To summarize: red or scarlet typifies the fact that Jesus was human and that He was the Son of Man. Here is a great contrast then:

Blue .... Divinity .... Jesus, the Son of God.
Scarlet ...... Humanity .... Jesus, the Son of Man.

And now, between the two, comes a new color, blending them into each other with wonderful harmony. It is . . .

Purple. We all know how to secure this color in paint. It is by mixing blue and red. If we take the divine and the human in Christ and blend them, what have we? A Mediator. "There is one . . . Mediator between God and men, the Man Christ Jesus" (1 Tim. 2:5). The mediatorial glory of Christ as revealed in the purple is gone into in detail in my book *These Are the Garments*—which examines the high priest's robes. For this reason we leave it here.

Fine Linen served as the background for the colors; and how could Christ be all that He was, and accomplish all that He did, unless He was holy, perfect, pure, spotless, faultless, like the fine flour of the meal offering! Here, then, we see Christ as the sinless One.

With Cherubim. Cherubim speak to us of protection. We see them at the gate of the Garden of Eden, guarding the way to the Tree of Life; and above the mercy seat, guarding, seemingly, the sprinkled blood. In the ten inner curtains they become part of the ornamentation of the ceiling of the tabernacle. The priest, looking up, would be reminded that God's protecting forces were looking down.

Ten Curtains. Here is another point of interest. There were ten curtains, each twenty-eight cubits by four cubits. They were sewn together in two sets of five and then united by fifty golden clasps attached to one hundred blue loops, making the total dimensions twenty-eight cubits by forty cubits. Ten is an accepted typical number for division. A few instances revealing this fact are: the Ten Commandments, divided into two sections, one showing our duty toward God and the other our duty toward man; and so they were engraved on two tablets of stone. Ten virgins were divided in their outlook: five were wise, five were foolish. Ten fingers are divided on two hands. Ten toes are divided on two feet. And here are ten curtains divided into two fives. How does this apply to Christ? There are two aspects of truth here:

1. Christ is a divider of people. Matthew 10:34b–35, says: "I did not come to send peace but a sword. For I have come to set a man against his father. . . ." But the Christ who divides is the Christ who unites with the golden clasps of His love. He divides us from worldly associates and unites us to Himself; He divides us from the old life and links us with a new life, which is with Christ in God.

2. Christ came to divide the camp of the Enemy, calling out a people for Himself and linking them with God.

Fifty Golden Clasps. For the goats' hair curtains, you may recall, the clasps are of bronze, and they link together the hundred loops; but for these linen curtains the clasps are of gold. Here, then, is a progression such as can be noted everywhere in the tabernacle. The metals increase in value as we approach the center: bronze to gold.

When the curtains are in their place, forming the ceiling, the fifty clasps lie immediately above the golden band or strip that holds up the veil and divides the Holy of Holies from the Holy Place. Fifty, again, is the number of Pentecost. "And you shall count for yourselves from the day after the Sabbath, from the day that you brought the sheaf of the wave offering: seven Sabbaths shall be completed. Count fifty days to the day after the seventh Sabbath . . ." (Lev. 23:15–16). "Now when the Day of Pentecost had fully come . . ." (Acts 2:1). This was fifty days after Christ's resurrection. What happened then? The

Holy Spirit descended and sat upon each of the disciples, who were all filled with the power of the Holy Spirit. On that day the early disciples entered the dispensation of the Holy Spirit and of the Church. They surely could sing:

"I have passed the riven veil where the glories
never fail.
I am living in the presence of the King."

The fifty clasps prefigure all that Pentecost means. Pentecost in the Old Testament, Pentecost in the New Testament, surely implies Pentecost today.

CHAPTER 8

The Court and Gate

Exodus 27:9–19. Exodus 38:9–20.

"You shall also make the court of the tabernacle. For the south side there shall be hangings for the court woven of fine linen thread, one hundred cubits long for one side. And its twenty pillars and their twenty sockets shall be of bronze. The hooks of the pillars and their bands shall be of silver. Likewise along the length of the north side there shall be hangings one hundred cubits long, with its twenty pillars and their twenty sockets of bronze, and the hooks of the pillars and their bands of silver.

"And along with the width of the court on the west side shall be hangings of fifty cubits, with their ten pillars and their ten sockets. The width of the court on the east side shall be fifty cubits. The hangings on one side of the gate shall be fifteen cubits, with their three pillars and their three sockets. And on the other side shall be hangings of fifteen cubits, with their three pillars and their three sockets.

"For the gate of the court there shall be a screen twenty cubits long, woven of blue and purple and scarlet yarn, and fine linen thread, made by a weaver. It shall have four pillars and four sockets. All the pillars around the court shall have bands of silver; their hooks shall be of silver and their sockets of bronze. The length of the court shall be one hundred cubits, the width fifty throughout, and the height five cubits, woven of fine linen thread, and its sockets of bronze. All the utensils of the tabernacle for all its service, all its pegs, and all the pegs of the court, shall be of bronze." (Ex. 27:9–19)

THE COURT. This was a perfect oblong, twice as long as its breadth, being 100 cubits in length and 50 cubits in breadth; in English measure about 172 ft. long and 86 ft. wide, standing 8 ft. 6 in. high. Its perimeter consisted of sixty bronze pillars, possibly covering interiors of acacia wood (we are not actually told), set into sixty bronze sockets that were buried in the sand to be its foundation. Each pillar was topped with a capital overlaid with silver (Ex. 38:17), and also had a silver hook on which the curtains were hung. Standing apart at equal distances, there were twenty pillars on the south side, twenty on the north side, and ten on both the east and the west sides. These were joined to each other by silver connecting-rods called "bands" or "fillets" (A.V.). Each pillar was also secured by one or more cords fastened to bronze tent pegs (called "pins" in the A.V.). Upon these sixty pillars were hung 490 feet of fine linen fabric, while the gate portion was a 35-foot screen woven of blue and purple and scarlet yarn and fine linen thread. This made a complete enclosure.

The 35 feet of colored fabric, being in the center of the east end of the court, became the gate of entrance. This screen hung from four of the pillars.

What was the purpose of this curtain-rimmed

court? It had several.

1. *It was a barrier*. It prevented unlawful approach to the sacred building, thus preserving its sanctity.

2. *It was a protection*. It kept wild animals at a distance.

3. *It was a distinct line of demarcation*. It kept the camp outside and the tabernacle inside. A great lesson is to be learned here. God has called for a positive mark of separation between the Church and the world. Man desires to break down this barrier and mix the world and the Church; yet at the same time he seeks to set up very high barriers of sectarianism and denominationalism. The difference is that God has put the barrier between the world and the Church and called for a life of separation, but man has moved it and put it between himself and fellow believers, thus breaking the fellowship of saints.

4. *It was to create a way of approach*. Man cannot come as he thinks. There is but *one* way. God has provided it, and only by that way shall we ever approach God. That way is fully revealed as we study the furniture within.

While the Holy Place of the tabernacle was for priests only and the Holy of Holies excluded all but the high priest, yet within the court all who would could come—priest and layman alike, those of high and low degree, the young and old, the rich and the poor. The reason is that it was the place of *sacrifice*, and all needed its efficacy—for without the shedding of blood there was no remission.

Just a word as to the typology of the court. It was a wonderful exhibition of righteousness. How the white linen of that court must have stood out in contrast to all the hundreds of black tents pitched on every side of it. It is surely a picture of Christ's righteousness in the midst of a perverse and crooked generation.

The court is a wonderful picture of the Word of God, for the Word reveals how sin has been judged and put underfoot (bronze sockets). It holds up as its head (silver capitals) the redemptive work of Christ and, at the same time, displays on every hand the righteousness of God.

The theme of redemption, running through the whole Bible, is sometimes called "the scarlet thread of redemption," "the hallmark of safety." Here it is seen as the silver band of redemption, extending to the full measurement of the court.

From whatever direction man seeks to approach God, the law of God both *demands* holiness and *exhibits* holiness. Man is not holy and cannot meet its demands, and so the curtains say: "Not this way." Does that drive man away—a hopeless, helpless creature? Not at all. Paul says: "The law was our tutor to bring us to Christ," and so the curtains lead the sinner around until he comes to an entrance of blue, purple, and scarlet, on a background of righteousness. That entrance is Christ, the only One who satisfied the claims of the law. He is the One who said, "I am the way, the truth, and the life. No man comes to the Father except through Me" (John 14:6). In His righteousness I find my approach. What a picture! What a truth! ! What a Savior! ! ! But having been brought thus far, let us consider . . .

The Gate. It has much to teach us concerning the same Great Person and the same great work to whom and to which all types point, and of which the tabernacle is a masterpiece of typology.

1. It was an only gate. Jesus said, "I am the way." How definite and decisive are the words of the Lord. There is but one way of salvation. If the Lord had said "I am *a* way," we might have considered other ways. If He had said "You *may* be born again," we could have asked: "What else may we do." But no! He is definite—*The* way, *must* be born again. All who seek to enter in by other ways or by other means are thieves and robbers.

2. It was a wide gate. Thirty-five feet wide. It was wide enough to receive "whosoever will"; but with all its width, entrance was still limited to a gate and restricted to a way. It is of interest to note that it was the same overall size as both the door of the tabernacle and the veil dividing the two chambers, although it was not the same shape. Each of the three measured a hundred square cubits. This gate had the breadth of universal access, for all *may* come although few do come. The other entrances had increased height, which speaks of exalted spiritual experience.

3. It was an accessible gate. How often we see gates and doors that are nearly always barred and bolted, opened only on special occasions and perhaps only for special people. There are also some gates that require a porter to open them. For instance, the gate of church membership is sometimes overly constricted by doctrinal niceties or by man-made rules and regulations. How different is the gate of God's providing. This gate is of a strong fabric, yet it is easy to open: a child can push back a curtain; the aged can find access; the weak or the unlearned are not debarred—for all know how to open so easy a gate.

One thing must be emphasized here. Sometimes you will see pictures or diagrams that show this gate beautifully looped back and fastened on either side, or else rolled up and made secure on the lintel above. This surely must be wrong. If it were thus folded, why have a gate at all? Any wild animal could roam in; any person could accidentally stroll through. Alas, we see parallels to this constantly in everyday life. We meet church members who have become such quite by chance—they are "Christians" simply because they were born into a Christian family. This can easily be a condition of self-deception, not salvation. No, the gate was closed—but it was not locked. It merely required the putting forth of one's hand and the pushing back of the screen. Even so with our great salvation! I appeal to you, my reader: Have you reached out the hand of faith and had personal contact with God, saying: "O Lamb of God, I come"? Conversion is not an accident; it is a real and definite personal experience.

4. *It was an attractive gate.* Its wonderful blend of colors, standing out in beautiful contradistinction to the clear whiteness of the curtains, must have attracted the onlooker. Even so the glorious attributes of Christ stand out as a lovely relief from the holy demands of the law of God. The symbolism of these colors we have considered in the previous chapter, so a summary here will suffice:

Blue .... The Son of God satisfying the demands of God.

Purple .... The Kinsman-Redeemer, bringing God and man together.

Scarlet ...... The Son of Man meeting the needs of man.

Linen .... His holy character, making it possible for Him to open on our behalf a new and living way.

5. *It was a well-supported gate.* Four pillars upheld the fabric, so manifesting its full beauty. Mention has been made of the pillars of the court as representing the Word of God, holding forth God's righteous demands. May not these four pillars be designated as the representation of Matthew, Mark, Luke, and John, who show us much of the character, work, glory, and life of Christ? Matthew makes much of the purple as he portrays the Royal King. Mark sees more of the scarlet and tells us of a suffering servant. Luke surely reveals the white linen of the perfect man from heaven. John ever remains the one to point to the blue and say: "Behold, the Lamb of God!"

A final word—this gate will remain open as long as the Day of Grace remains. It is Christ, and He said, "If any one enters by Me, he will be saved." The gate is the first step. It is the step of decision. Man today is undecided, but decision must come before acceptance, as repentance must come before forgiveness.

· Chapter 9 ·

The Pillar of Cloud and Fire

Exodus 13:20–22. Exodus 40:33–38. Numbers 9:15–23.

And he raised up the court all around the tabernacle and the altar, and hung up the screen of the court gate. So Moses finished the work. Then the cloud covered the tabernacle of meeting, and the glory of the Lord filled the tabernacle. And Moses was not able to enter the tabernacle of meeting, because the cloud rested above it, and the glory of the Lord filled the tabernacle. When the cloud was taken up from above the tabernacle, the children of Israel went onward in all their journeys. But if the cloud was not taken up, then they did not journey till the day that it was taken up. For the cloud of the Lord was above the tabernacle by day, and fire was over it by night, in the sight of all the house of Israel, throughout all their journeys. (Ex. 40:33–38)

And on the day that the tabernacle was raised up, the cloud covered the tabernacle, the tent of the Testimony; from evening until morning it was above the tabernacle like the appearance of fire. So it was always: the cloud covered it by day, and the appearance of fire by night. Whenever the cloud was taken up from above the tabernacle, after that the children of Israel would journey; and in the place where the cloud settled, there the children of Israel would pitch their tents. At the command of the

Lord the children of Israel would journey, and at the command of the Lord they would camp; as long as the cloud stayed above the tabernacle they remained encamped. Even when the cloud continued long, many days above the tabernacle, the children of Israel kept the charge of the Lord and did not journey. So it was, when the cloud was above the tabernacle a few days: according to the command of the Lord they would remain encamped, and according to the command of the Lord they would journey. So it was, when the cloud remained only from evening until morning: when the cloud was taken up in the morning, then they would journey; whether by day or by night, whenever the cloud was taken up, they would journey. Whether it was two days, a month, or a year that the cloud remained above the tabernacle, the children would remain encamped and not journey; but when it was taken up, they would journey. At the command of the Lord they remained encamped, and at the command of the Lord they journeyed; they kept the charge of the Lord, at the command of the Lord by the hand of Moses. (Num. 9:15–23)

WE have made mention in a previous chapter of the sheik's spear and his use of it for command, observing that the pillar of cloud served similarly in the movements of the tabernacle and the camp. We will now glean some lessons from this "pillar of cloud by day and pillar of fire by night."

The origin of the pillar remains a mystery—for we have not been told how it came, only when it came. It is introduced to us in a very matter-of-fact way: "So they took their journey from Succoth and camped in Etham at the edge of the wilderness. And the Lord went before them by day in a pillar of a cloud to lead the way, and by night in a pillar of fire to give them light, so as to go by day and night. He did not take away the pillar of cloud by day or the pillar of fire by night from before the people" (Ex. 13:20–22).

The Typology. This pillar of cloud is a wonderful type of the incarnation of the Lord Jesus Christ. God was in this pillar to lead His people. "God was in Christ reconciling the world to Himself . . ." (2 Cor. 5:19). It was not just a hovering cloud but a pillar of cloud. A pillar stands as an emblem of strength and stability, like those pillars of Solomon's Temple. Christ was the strong one who was in the midst of His people. Not only was it a pillar of cloud but it was also a pillar of fire in the hours of darkness. So then, this symbol of the Divine Presence could never be erased. The "strong east wind" that blew all night and parted the waters of the Red Sea (Ex. 14:21) never blew this cloud across the sky. It remained, contrary to nature, "a pillar." The darkness of the storm cloud made it appear especially bright, yet the brightness of the sun could not dim it. It constantly stood out against its environment. No weather prophet could explain it, and no scientist could explain it away. What glorious truth! Is it not the same with our Divine Leader? The storm of opposition and persecution cannot hide His blessed face. The bright sunshine of success should not dim for us the glories of the Lord; and neither the skeptic, atheist, nor modernist with all their materialistic arguments or bitter attacks can alter the fact that the Lord is in the midst of His people leading them all the way.

WHAT WAS THIS PILLAR OF CLOUD TO ISRAEL? It was:

1. *A symbol of the presence of God.* From the time the symbol was given at Etham on the coast of the Red Sea until the tabernacle was built at Sinai, the pillar appeared to have no particular abiding place, for we read of it in various places. In Exodus 16:10, it was toward the wilderness: "Now it came to pass, as Aaron spoke to the whole congregation of the children of Israel, that they looked toward the wilderness, and behold, the glory of the Lord appeared in the cloud." In Exodus 33, the cloud appeared at the door of the tabernacle with Moses: "Moses took his tent and pitched it outside the camp, far from the camp, and called it the tabernacle of meeting. And it came to pass that every one who sought the Lord went out to the tabernacle of meeting which was outside the camp. So it was, whenever Moses went out to the tabernacle, that all the people rose, and each man stood at his tent door and watched Moses until he had gone into the tabernacle. And it came to pass, when Moses entered into the tabernacle, that the pillar of cloud descended and stood at the door of the tabernacle, and the Lord talked with Moses. All the people saw the pillar of cloud standing at the tabernacle door, and all the people rose and worshiped, each man in his tent door" (vv. 7–10).

It is quite evident that the tabernacle here referred to was not the tabernacle of the Lord which we are considering because, first of all, it was never outside the camp but always in the midst and, second, it was not Moses who entered into *the* tabernacle but Aaron. Thirdly, the tabernacle of the Lord was not yet built. This was a common tent that Moses used for sacred purposes prior to the construction of the tabernacle of the Lord. When the cloud descended upon this special tent it meant that God had come down to talk with Moses.

When the tabernacle was built and the glory of the Lord filled the place, then the pillar moved and took up its permanent abode over the ark of the covenant and the *Shekinah* glory. The pillar of cloud and fire then became the outward evidence to man of the inner glory of the Lord's presence.

2. Their guide. When it moved, they moved; when it rested, they rested. It mattered not whether it was for a day or a week, a month or even a year. This is stated in Numbers 9:15–23, quoted at the beginning of this chapter.

We learn from Israel's history that they often had to move at a moment's notice. Sometimes it was during the day and sometimes at night. Let us look at their first move as an illustration. They had reached the edge of the wilderness. They had not journeyed straight forward; a map of their travels indicates that the pillar had led them southward, and they found themselves in a place with mountains on either side of them and the Red Sea stretching itself right across their path, so that there was no way out. This caused Pharaoh to conclude: "They are bewildered and entangled in the land; they are an easy prey." It looked like God was driving the children of Israel to complete destruction. Actually He was leading Pharaoh and the Egyptians to their doom, for at the critical moment the pillar changed its position. How often the Christian has had such tests. But God is faithful—He does not fail.

On another occasion they were enduring the bitter experience of Marah, but God led them on to Elim. There they enjoyed the shade of the seventy palm trees and the refreshment of the twelve wells. That was a pleasant change. Surely they would stay awhile at Elim! But no, they were led right into the heart of the wilderness, with no food. But God's intent was for them to learn how He could provide when they could not. Indeed it is true that:

> "God moves in a mysterious way
> His wonders to perform;
> He plants His footsteps in the sea
> And rides upon the storm.
>
> "Deep in unfathomable mines
> Of never failing skill,
> He treasures up His bright designs
> And works His sovereign will."

3. *Their protection.* At the time when they appeared to have been led into a trap at the Red Sea, the pillar moved from before them as a vanguard to take up its position behind as a rear guard. In so doing, it came between them and their enemies, being to the one a source of help and blessing and to the

other a cause of defeat. How much is this like the cross of Christ! The cross certainly stands between the believer and the world. To the believer, the cross symbolizes his salvation; to the rejecter, it symbolizes his condemnation. In this position the pillar became light to God's people and thick darkness to His enemies. That brings us to our next point.

4. *Their source of light.* Have you ever considered that, apart from this pillar, this great caravan of people had no light. They were in the wilderness. We talk about the modern inventions of our day and include floodlighting as one of them, but here was the first floodlighting effect. The pillar of fire stood at the Red Sea and floodlit the path that God had made through the waters. This pillar was God's presence. "God is light," and "if we walk in the light as He is in the light, we have fellowship with one another . . ." (1 John 1:5,7).

5. *Their shelter.* The pillar appears to have opened out over the people like a great umbrella. The psalmist infers this, for he says: "He spread a cloud for a covering, and fire to give light in the night" (Ps. 105:39). So the sun shall not smite *you* by day nor the moon by night. And yet again the psalmist writes: "He who dwells in the secret place of the Most High shall abide under the shadow of the Almighty" (Ps. 91:1). Our shelter at all times is the blood of Christ. Finally:

6. *It is to be restored.* "Then the Lord will create above every dwelling place of Mount Zion, and above her assemblies, a cloud and smoke by day and the shining of a flaming fire by night. For over all the

glory there will be a covering. And there will be a tabernacle for shade in the daytime from the heat, for a place of refuge, and for a shelter from storm and rain" (Isa. 4:5–6).

This is a prophetic utterance!

CHAPTER 10

The Bronze Altar

Exodus 27:1–8. Exodus 38:1–7. Exodus 20:24–26.

"You shall make an altar of acacia wood, five cubits long and five cubits broad—the altar shall be square— and its height shall be three cubits. You shall make its horns on its four corners; its horns shall be of one piece with it. And you shall overlay it with bronze. Also you shall make its pans to receive its ashes, and its shovels and its basins and its forks and its firepans; you shall make all its utensils of bronze. You shall make a grate for it, a network of bronze; and on the network you shall make four bronze rings at its four corners. You shall put it under the rim of the altar beneath, that the network may be midway up the altar. And you shall make poles for the altar, poles of acacia wood, and overlay them with bronze. The poles shall be put in the rings, and the poles shall be on the two sides of the altar to bear it. You shall make it hollow with boards; as it was shown you on the mountain, so shall they make it." (Ex. 27:1–8)

WE have now come in our studies to the furniture of the tabernacle, every piece of which is charged with meaning and stands to declare the plans and purposes of God. Upon entering the gate of the court we are confronted with the first and largest piece of furniture, namely, the bronze altar. The critic might say that animal sacrifices savor of heathenism, but one needs to remember that the heathen do half-follow truth. Sacrifice is God ordained. It was an absolute essential to Jewish worship. God must have taught something in connection with sacrifice to our foreparents when He made them tunics of skin. The offerings of Cain and Abel were a demonstration of a possessed knowledge of altar building in connection with worship. It is interesting to note that, after the deluge, Noah built an altar before he built a house (Genesis 8:18–20) and that Abram built an altar wherever he pitched a tent (Genesis 12:7–8). Even so must we ourselves visit the "altar" and see our "Sacrifice" dying for us before we can step into any blessing of a Christian walk or know anything of the fellowship of a living Christ.

A word as to its . . .

Meaning. The Hebrew word for altar is *mizbeach,* meaning "slaughter place." That is why, as we have just seen, the altar plays such an important part. That is also why it stands in such a prominent position. The law declares that without the shedding of blood there is no remission. As to the use of the altar, we learn that it lifted up the sacrifice in smoke; at the same time, it would lift the offerer up into fellowship with God. And later, when the cross became the altar for the world's greatest sacrifice, it lifted up Christ. We gaze on it and sing:

"Lifted up was He to die,
  'It is finished' was His cry;
  Now in heaven, exalted high:
  Hallelujah! What a Saviour!"

"And I, if I am lifted up from the earth, will draw all peoples to Myself" (John 12:32). The altar had but one . . .

Purpose. Upon it sacrifices were to be consumed, so meeting and satisfying the claims of God. As a holy God, He has irrevocable claims which must be fully realized before He can show forth mercy; sin must be punished, either in person or through a substitute. The lamb, goat, bull, etc., were Israel's substitutes, and God accepted them by means of the altar. These great claims of God have since been met to the full in Christ at Calvary, when He became the Offering, the Altar, and the Priest. Many types, metaphors, names, etc., are used to give expression to the all-sufficiency of Christ, who has met man's tremendous need from every conceivable angle.

Upon entering the court our attention is naturally drawn to the . . .

Position of the altar, just inside the gate—easily accessible, unavoidable, and unmistakable to the truly penitent inquirer. The altar was not inside the tabernacle but inside the court. It stood at the gate of repentance. Repentance is not salvation, it is only sorrow for sin. When a sinner comes to the place where he realizes he is a sinner, he must be not only sorry for that sin but also willing to turn his back on it. Then it is he sees, standing before him, the altar:

> "And there before him stands the cross,
> Two arms outstretched to save,
> Like a watchman set to guard the way
> From that eternal grave."

Many people see in the altar the *end* of things. This is only partially true. It *is* the end of the *old* life. It is the "It is finished" of Christ's redeeming work. On the other hand, it is the *beginning* of a holy walk and one's Christian experience. The altar, then, is only the first step in a new walk.

Let us now turn our attention to the altar's . . .

Size. Five by five by three cubits. It was decidedly the largest piece of furniture. It has been said that all the other furniture could be put within its compass! Whether this was literally so or not, seeing that two pieces have no stated size, remains a question. But of one thing we are sure—that every future blessing and the many spiritual applications of the other furniture are certainly within the fold of Calvary; and *all* is ours because Christ's death has made them so. Five cubits square! Five is the number of Grace. Hallelujah! It is all of grace, the unmerited favor of God toward a sinful world. Such grace holds no whims or fancies, no partiality or favoritism. It is square, an emblem of solidity and equality. The three cubits high might suggest to us that it was the third day when our great Sacrifice was accepted by a satisfied Jehovah who demonstrated His approval by raising Christ from the dead.

We must not overlook the . . .

Materials employed, although they have come under our observation before. They were acacia wood and bronze. The acacia tree grew with great profusion on and around Sinai, where the tabernacle was built. This reminds us that the humanity of Christ—of which wood is the symbol—was an *ordinary* humanity, not a specially prepared body that was exempt from suffering. "Inasmuch then as the children have partaken of flesh and blood, He Himself likewise shared in the same, that through death He might destroy him who had the power of death, that is, the devil" (Heb. 2:14). This wood was strengthened by an overlay of bronze; it was strengthened for endurance. Had not Christ been strengthened by His Father He would never have been able to endure. His mental and physical weakness were seen in such places as Gethsemane when He sweat great drops of blood and on the cross when He said, "I thirst!" and "My God, My God, why have You forsaken Me?" (Jn. 19:28; Mk. 15:34).

Bronze is not a precious metal like silver or gold; rather, it is an alloy of copper and tin, both common metals. (Brass too is an alloy, of copper and zinc. Brass, however, was unknown at that time; so the word "brass," found throughout in the Authorized Version, is a mistranslation of the Hebrew word *nechosheth*.)

Some people have criticized the fact that the altar was constructed of wood overlaid with metal; they suggest that heated metal would burn the wood. A few years ago, however, at a time when Britain was seeking to conserve metal, a "discovery" was made by some scientists. They concluded that a door made of wood and overlaid with copper, the joints of which were hammered so that they were hermetically sealed, was absolutely *fireproof*. The invention was delivered to the London County Council Fire Brigade, who put it through their tests. It stood them all and was certified "fireproof." This was considered a "modern invention," but it certainly answers the dispute about the bronze altar. Not only that, it stands as another witness to the accuracy of the Bible and reveals that the Bible is ahead of science and not contrary to it.

Our attention is now drawn to the . . .

Design, the outstanding feature of which is the grate. It is generally accepted that the bronze grate had its position about halfway-down inside. This theory I wish to refute, first on grounds of the logic of the context, and second on the demands of the law concerning the altars of Israel.

1. The context. Let us read it very carefully. "You shall make a grate for it, a network of bronze; and on the network you shall make four bronze rings at its four corners. You shall put it under the rim of the altar beneath, that the network may be midway up the altar. And you shall make poles for the altar, poles of acacia wood, and overlay them with bronze. The poles shall be put in the rings, and the poles shall be on the two sides of the altar to bear it" (Ex. 27:4–7). The Hebrew word for grate is *makber*, which is derived from the root word *kabar* meaning "to twist" or "to plait together," and is used only here. *Makber* does not mean a sieve, as some suggest. This grate was put *under* the rim of the altar. The word rim ("compass"—A.V.) literally means "surrounding band," or that which encircles the outside. I am suggesting that this band was a shelf on which to keep the utensils mentioned in verse 3. This detail is immaterial except to further suggest that it surrounded the *outside* halfway up—"midway"—that is, a cubit and a half from the top and a cubit and a half from the bottom. To put the grate under this band ("ledge"—NIV) must mean to put it outside. Again, four rings are to be put in the four corners or "extremities" (*qatsah*) of the grate, and through these rings, which were on the two sides of the altar, the staves were to pass. This could not be done if the grate were inside. Furthermore, the reference says "You shall make it hollow with boards." To be hollow, the altar must be void of anything inside. This again places the grating outside. On what, then, was the offering made? This brings us to our next point.

2. *What the law demanded.* We are told in Exodus 20:24–26, "An altar of earth you shall make for Me, and you shall sacrifice on it your burnt offerings and your peace offerings, your sheep and your oxen. In every place where I record My name I will come to you, and I will bless you. And if you make Me an altar of stone, you shall not build it of hewn stone; for if you use your tool on it, you have profaned it. Nor shall you go up by steps to My altar, that your nakedness may not be exposed on it." This scripture would make it quite unlawful to offer a sacrifice on a grate, because it would have been tooled. It also sug-

gests that the bronze altar was a case that would be filled inside with earth or unhewn stone whenever the tabernacle was pitched. All this evidence puts the grating on the *outside* of the altar, hanging beneath the rim.

The question is naturally asked: "Why was it there?" We are informed that the altar possessed four horns, and to these the sacrificial animals were tied. There is a natural revulsion to the smell of blood and death, and a resistance on the part of the animal would take place—the mode of resistance being to kick. This grating of bronze surrounding the lower portion of the altar would therefore protect the altar from damage. Cannot we see the application? Bring the critic, the modernist, the atheist to the altar of Calvary; speak to him of sacrifice and the shedding of blood; endeavor to tie him to the truth of God's Word—and he will immediately kick against the blood, denying its efficacy. But, blessed be God, Calvary is surrounded by the Holy Spirit. Let them kick as they will; they can do no harm. On the other hand, the believer is called to yield himself as a *willing* sacrifice, not a resisting one.

So much for the altar except a further word on . . .

The Horns. These were a unique feature of Israelitish altars. These projections were four in number, one at each corner. As symbols of power and authority they pointed to the four corners of the earth. The horn of salvation, provided through the sacrifice of Calvary, points to every corner of the earth, saving to the uttermost, for:

"Red and yellow, brown and white,
   All are precious in His sight.
   Jesus died for all the peoples of the world."

Sacrifices were bound to the horns of the altar of burnt offering because of their unwillingness. The psalmist refers to such an action: "Bind the sacrifice with cords to the horns of the altar" (Ps. 118:27b).

Our Sacrifice was bound to the altar of the cross by the cords of love. This is so beautifully expressed by A.M. Kelly:

"Was it the nails, O Saviour, that bound Thee to
      the tree?
   Nay! 'Twas Thine everlasting Love, Thy love for
      me, for me."

Then in turn you must "present your bodies a living sacrifice, holy, acceptable to God, which is your reasonable service" (Rom. 12:1).

One or two brief reflections upon the appurtenances and the ritual. In this connection the number five repeats itself, in five utensils, five animals, and five offerings—standing out as further evidence of the grace that abounds at the altar. The five utensils were:

The Pans. These were used for the ashes, which are to be referred to again in a moment.

The Shovels. Their use was for picking up the ashes, and for tending or feeding the fire.

The Basins. They held the blood of the sacrifice, which was sometimes carried inside and sometimes poured out at the foot of the altar.

The Forks. These were for the arranging of the sacrifice in order on the wood.

The Firepans (actually the "censers") were used for carrying the fire of the altar. With such censers Nadab and Abihu offered profane fire before the Lord and died (Lev. 10:1–2). When the plague broke out because of the rebellion of Korah, Dathan and Abiram, Moses said to Aaron, "Take a censer [firepan] and put fire in it from the altar, put incense on it, and take it quickly to the congregation and make atonement for them; for wrath has gone out from the Lord. The plague has begun" (Num. 16:46).

The five animals mentioned were the lamb, goat, bull, heifer, and turtle dove. Leviticus records the five offerings in connection with the altar of burnt offering. They were the burnt offering, the grain offering, the peace offering, the sin offering, and the trespass offering—a subject we must enter into separately in future studies.

The concluding word is on the ritual of the ashes and the blood. First,

The Ashes. But surely these were just thrown away! No, not according to the law of the burnt offering. It stipulated that "the priest shall put on his linen garment, and his linen trousers he shall put upon his body, and take up the ashes of the burnt offering which the fire has consumed on the altar, and he shall put them beside the altar. Then he shall take off his garments, put on other garments, and carry the ashes outside the camp to a clean place" (Lev. 6:10–11). We shall not deal with the ceremony here, but with the ashes themselves. They were the last to be seen of the sacrifice—they were a proof that the sacrifice was accepted; so with solemn rites they were deposited in a clean place, afterwards to be used for the ceremonial cleansing of the unclean as recorded in Numbers 19. Even so, when we come to the world's great altar and the world's greatest offering—Calvary—we find that the evidence of the completeness of the work was the taking down of the body (the ashes) and placing it in a new tomb in which man had never lain (the clean place), from which He arose to cleanse the sinner. To this the apostle referred when he said: "How much more shall the blood of Christ . . . purge your conscience from dead works to serve the living God" (Heb. 9:14). Lastly we consider . . .

The Blood. It was never used, but was poured out at the bottom of the altar. Man must not use blood or partake of it, because the life is in the blood; thus the blood poured out was a further evidence and a second witness to the fact that the life was poured out. When Christ gave His life, He gave His all. "Though He was rich, yet for your sakes He became poor, that you through His poverty might become rich" (2 Cor. 8:9b). How poor He became! How rich we become!

· Chapter 11 ·

The Bronze Laver

Exodus 30:17–21. Exodus 38:8. Exodus 40:7.

Then the Lord spoke to Moses, saying: "You shall also make a laver of bronze, with its base also of bronze, for washing. You shall put it between the tabernacle of meeting and the altar. And you shall put water in it, for Aaron and his sons shall wash their hands and their feet in water from it. When they go into the tabernacle of meeting, or when they come near the altar to minister, to burn an offering made by fire to the Lord, they shall wash with water, lest they die. So they shall wash their hands and their feet, lest they die. And it shall be a statute forever to them—to him and his descendants throughout their generations." (Ex. 30:17–21)

He made the laver of bronze and its base of bronze, from the bronze mirrors of the serving women who assembled at the door of the tabernacle of meeting. (Ex. 38:8)

VERY little is recorded concerning this piece of furniture, and yet how important an item it is! It would almost appear to be enshrouded in mystery. No statement is made concerning its shape or size, and when we read of the furniture being covered and conveyed, the laver is never mentioned. In coming to such a subject we realize we are approaching the subject of sanctification, a matter so little understood and concerning which there are such variant doctrinal views. Let us consider first:

Its Origin. The laver was made from the bronze mirrors of the women of Israel. It was their freewill offering, and we have every reason to believe that it was a sacrifice on their part, even as it would be to many today. But then, what are gifts unless they really cost us something!

One wonders sometimes why it was that they chose to give their mirrors rather than something else. We could easily say that a mirror is an essential to a neat and tidy person, and God never desires untidyness; but we have no reason to believe that they became mirrorless. Might it not be that they had caught a vision of themselves as God saw them—something which caused them to realize that the adornment of inward character was far more important than wasting time adorning the outer person which is ready to perish?

It is interesting to notice how often we get a glimpse of New Testament truth in inspired actions of Old Testament people. Our mind travels to 1 Timothy 2:9–10: "In like manner also, [I desire] that the women adorn themselves in modest apparel, with propriety and moderation, not with braided hair or gold or pearls or costly clothing, but, which is proper for women professing godliness, with good works." And again to 1 Peter 3:3–4: "Do not let your beauty be that outward adorning of arranging the hair, of wearing gold, or of putting on fine apparel; but let it be the hidden person of the heart, with the incorruptible ornament of a gentle and quiet spirit, which is very precious in the sight of God." There are but two ways of seeing ourselves: first, in our own mirrors, where we have quite a good opinion of ourselves and yet a desire ever to improve our appearance; the other, in the light and mirror of God's Word, where we see ourselves as God sees us, that is, unclean—so that we say with Isaiah: "Woe is me, for I am undone . . ." (Isa. 6:5).

Its Form. It is often stated that nothing is said on this matter, but a little consideration will show that enough is said to enlighten the eyes of our understanding—and enough is *not* said to give us food for thought. We all know such sayings as "Actions speak louder than words" and "Silence is golden." The silences of Scripture often speak very clearly and loudly and are very precious.

"A laver with its base"—that is the only description; but there is possibly more in "its base" than that which appears in casual reading. It does not say a "pedestal," but a "base" or "foot" (A.V.). This could be any shape. I am very strongly of the opinion that it was in the form of a shallow bowl. A large upper reservoir was the laver proper and a wide, shallow bowl the foot, the two possibly being connected by a pedestal. Now as to the reason for such a design.

Middle Eastern people do not wash in a bowl or basin, but always in running water if at all possible. Ewers and basins are commonly used for washing the hands and feet, the method being to hold the

hands or the feet over the basin and then to pour
the water from the ewer. Recent excavations at Ur
of the Chaldees have brought to light an early bath,
very shallow, with an inlet and outlet for water. The
bather would lie flat and allow the water to flow
through, thus cleaning him. It has been pointed out
also that a fountain stands in the court of one of the
mosques at Jerusalem to which the Moslems come
for their daily ablutions. This is fitted with taps from
which the water runs into a lower basin and thence
drains away. To all this we shall add an extract from
the pen of the late John Kitto in his notes in the
Pictorial Bible:

> Our impression is that the laver, whatever its
> shape, stood upon another basin, more wide and
> shallow, as a cup on a saucer; and that the latter
> received, from cocks or spouts in the upper basin,
> the water which was allowed to escape when the
> priests washed themselves with the water which
> fell from the upper basin. If by the under basin we
> understand the "foot" of the text, the sense is clear.
> The text does not say that the priests were to
> wash themselves *in* the basin, but *at* it. *In* it they
> could not well wash their hands and feet if the
> laver was of any height. The Rabbins say the la-
> ver had several cocks, or "nipples," as they call
> them, from which the water was let out as wanted.
> There were several such spouts, but the number is
> differently stated.

Just how the priests washed their hands and
feet at the laver seems uncertain. That they did

not wash *in* either the laver or its basin seems clear, because then the water in which they washed would have been rendered impure by those who washed before or with them—and we know that Orientals do not like to wash in a basin after our manner, in which the water with which we commence washing is clearer than that with which we finish, but at a falling stream, where each successive affusion is of clean water. So we are inclined to think that the priests either washed themselves with the stream as it fell from the spouts into the base, or else received in proper vessels as much water as they needed for the occasion.

The Orientals, in their washings, make use of a vessel with a long spout and wash at the stream which issues from thence, the waste water being received into a basin which is placed underneath. This seems to us to illustrate the idea of the laver with its base, as well as the ablutions of the priests. The laver had thus its upper basin, from which the stream fell, and the under basin for receiving the waste water. It is quite compatible with the same idea and practice to suppose that, to prevent too great an expenditure of water, they received a quantity in separate vessels, using it as described, and the base received the water which in washing fell from their hands and feet. This explanation, although it seems to us probable, is, necessarily, only conjectural.

The Jewish commentators say that any kind of water might be used for the laver, but that it was to be changed every day. They also state that ab-

lution before entering the tabernacle was in no
case dispensed with. A man might be perfectly
clean, might be quite free from any ceremonial
impurity, and might even have washed his hands
and feet before he left home, but still he could by
no means enter the tabernacle without previously
washing at the laver.

The evidence is almost conclusive that this was the
form of the laver in the tabernacle of Israel.

Its Position. It was in the court where the priests
ministered daily in sacrifices. It stood between the
altar and the tabernacle. It was independent of the
altar in position, but dependent on it for the blood
that was sprinkled: "Likewise he [Moses] sprinkled
with blood both the tabernacle and all the vessels of
the ministry. And according to the law almost all
things are purged with blood . . ." (Heb. 9:21–22). It
is important to note this relationship of the laver to
the altar because of its doctrinal import, which we
shall consider under our next heading.

Its Type. After the aforesaid, maybe we shall be
privileged to take up a new trend of thought from
the customary one of the laver being a type of the
Holy Spirit. Admittedly, this is rather premature.
We shall meet truths concerning the Holy Spirit
later, when we enter the tabernacle.

The Spirit is for those who have clean hands and
clean feet. John says: ". . . the Holy Spirit was not
yet given, because Jesus was not yet glorified" (John
7:39). What is it that stands out so preeminently
and yet so many have failed to see it just here? The

laver symbolizes the Word of God. May we consider this from the points of view before us.

First, the laver was made from mirrors. It revealed man to himself, and "by the *law* is the knowledge of sin" (Rom. 3:20b). The Word reveals our inability to live the Christian life in our own strength. The Word reveals much more. "For if anyone is a hearer of the word and not a doer, he is like a man observing his natural face in a mirror; for he observes himself, goes away, and immediately forgets what kind of man he was. But he who looks into the perfect law of liberty and continues in it, and is not a forgetful hearer but a doer of the work, this one will be blessed in what he does" (James 1:23–25).

Second, the laver also provided the necessary cleansing. Here lies possibly the greatest importance of its position, namely, beyond the altar. The altar was accessible to all, the laver only to the priests. The altar with its sacrifices was to deal with the subject of sin, but the laver was for those for whom atonement had been made. The Lord said to Peter, "He who is bathed needs only to wash his feet, but is completely clean . . ." (John 13:10). At the altar of Calvary the sinner was bathed, for "the blood of Jesus Christ His Son cleanses us from *all* sin" (1 John 1:7b). At the laver the believer finds his daily cleansing from the defilements of life. He is thereby enabled to live a sanctified life.

The life of holiness is made possible by the Word of God; therefore, may we stress the fact that the laver is a type of the Word of God rather than of the Holy Spirit, who dwells inside our "tabernacle" working to produce the sanctified life. The best way to clinch this aspect of truth will be to quote the Word and so let it speak for itself:

"*Sanctify* them by Your truth. Your *word is* truth" (John 17:17).

"How can a young man *cleanse* his way? By taking heed according to Your *word*" (Ps. 119:9).

"That He might *sanctify* and *cleanse* it with the washing of water by the *word*" (Eph. 5:26).

"You are already *clean* because of the *word* which I have spoken to you" (John 15:3).

You will, of course, observe that these references all apply to the believer. The unbeliever is always exhorted to find his cleansing in the blood of Christ.

Finally, may we briefly note . . .

The Instructions. "For Aaron and his sons shall wash their hands and their feet in water from it. When they go into the tabernacle of meeting, or when they come near the altar to minister, to burn an offering made by fire to the Lord, they shall wash with water, lest they die. So they shall wash their hands and their feet, lest they die" (Ex. 30:19–21a).

Those who minister before the Lord must be clean. It was not a matter of opinion but a case of necessity. The priest had to wash every time he ministered, thus teaching us that one act can defile and make us unfit for service. Bearing in mind that we have taken the laver as a type of the Word of God, we have a great lesson to learn. It matters not whether we are going inside to minister to the Lord's people or whether we are going to the cross to point someone to the great sacrifice for sin, we must ourselves first go to the Word and see that we who bear the vessels of the Lord are clean. So many of the Lord's people have such a lack of knowledge and are so unacquainted with the words of Scripture that they misquote, misinterpret, or adulterate them with their own ideas and fancies, and thus their ministry is anything but clean and their life anything but "set apart" or sanctified. The result is that though—being under grace—they do not die as was demanded by the law, yet their works are certainly dead. One needs to be well acquainted with both the Author and the Book if anything in the way of a lasting and a God-glorifying work is to be accomplished.

" I'm acquainted with the Author and I know God's Word is true,
   In times of grief it brings relief, and tells me what to do.
   Oh! I dearly love its pages, for I've found the Rock of Ages,
   I'm acquainted with the Author and I know 'tis true."

CHAPTER 12

The Golden Lampstand

Exodus 25:31–40; 37:17–24; 39:37. Jeremiah 52:19.
Daniel 5:2–5. Revelation 1:12,20.

"You shall also make a lampstand of pure gold; the lampstand shall be of hammered work. Its shaft, its branches, its bowls, its ornamental knobs, and flowers shall be of one piece. And six branches shall come out of its sides: three branches of the lampstand out of one side, and three branches of the lampstand out of the other side. Three bowls shall be made like almond blossoms on one branch, with an ornamental knob and a flower, and three bowls made like almond blossoms on the other branch, with an ornamental knob and a flower—and so for the six branches that come out of the lampstand. On the lampstand itself four bowls shall be made like almond blossoms, each with its ornamental knob and flower. And there shall be a knob under the first two branches of the same, a knob under the second two branches of the same, and a knob under the third two branches of the same, according to the six branches that extend from the lampstand. Their knobs and their branches shall be of one piece; all of it shall be one hammered piece of pure gold. You shall make seven lamps for it, and they shall arrange its lamps so that they give light in front of it. And its wick-trimmers and their trays shall be of pure gold. It shall be made of a talent of pure gold, with all these utensils. And see to it that you make them according to the pattern which was shown you on the mountain." (Ex. 25:31–40)

WE have now to examine the furniture of the Holy Place. Passing through the door, to which reference will be made later, we leave behind bronze for gold, external for internal. The eye would naturally be drawn first toward the lampstand that stands to the left in the building. What a contrast! From a piece of furniture with practically no description to a menorah with details that are profuse!

Perhaps you are using the Authorized Version of the Bible, where the word used is "candlestick." By way of introduction may I say that it was not a candlestick according to the modern use of that word. The Middle Eastern folk of that day had only little clay lamps that burned olive oil. When in use these would be set on a tripod or three-legged stand. It is best to call that a lampstand. This we must bear in mind when reading Matthew 5:15 (A.V.): "Neither do men light a candle, and put it under a bushel, but *on* a candlestick; and it giveth light unto all that are in the house."

It is most obvious that the "candlestick" of the tabernacle is a lampstand, because the lamps are referred to—also their trimming. We would stress this point as we open the chapter because there is nothing in Scripture to warrant the use of candles in worship. The system practiced by some is absolutely erroneous and entirely foreign to the Word of God. Candles give light by the consumption of themselves, but the lamp gives its light by means of oil poured into it from time to time.

Let us examine this piece of furniture minutely. It was made of solid gold. Its weight was a talent, about 125 lb.; the value of that amount of gold was about $30,000 at our present standard. This does not include the cost of any labor put into it. Before we consider all the details given, let me state that it consisted of a main shaft out of which emerged seven branches, three to the right, three to the left, and one directly out of the top. There is no mention of a base, possibly because it was considered part of the shaft.

Now let us meditate upon . . .

Its Formation. "The lampstand shall be of hammered work." The lampstand—the most beautiful, the most complex, the most ornamental of all the pieces of furniture—was not cast in a mold; neither was it made in sections and assembled together, but it was beaten into its form and beauty out of a solid block of gold—a task which we are given to understand cannot be done today. Oh, the majesty of God's plans foreshadowed in type! What a picture of the unity of Christ with His Church! Could man do it today? Could man do it at all? What would you and I see in a nugget of gold? Just gold, that is all. What did Bezaleel see in it? We can fully appreciate that Bezaleel and his workmen were "anointed with the Spirit of God for all manner of artistic workmanship." He must have had divine revelation and guidance.

Ask a man like Michaelangelo what he sees in a

block of marble and we might hear him say: "Beautiful! Lovely! I see there a group of angels, I see a lovely figure, I see art!" But we say: "Where? We can see only crudeness." Then he uses his mallet, his chisels, and his *master mind,* and he begins—chip, chip, chip—knocking a piece off here, carving a piece out there, hard blows, light taps, till after a long process we begin to see what he saw all the time. That is how a statue comes into being; that was how the menorah made its appearance.

That was how the Church of God came to be. The Apostle Paul says: ". . . just as He chose us in Him before the foundation of the world, that we should be holy and without blame before Him in love . . ." (Eph. 1:4); while John speaks of ". . . the Lamb slain from the foundation of the world" (Rev. 13:8). Long before man saw the light of day, God saw the Church as a beautiful body of believers "without spot or wrinkle or any such thing." Long before man sinned, God in His foreknowledge planned our salvation in Christ: "For whom He foreknew, He also predestined to be conformed to the image of His Son" (Rom. 8:29). Such a truth ought to make one shout for joy. We are not "linked on"—not an afterthought—but one *in* Him and *with* Him: eternally and essentially a part of Him by sovereign grace. Surely this is eternal security! While God had thus planned it in His purposes, it was not seen until Pentecost and not revealed in its fullness until Paul saw it and said: "This is a great mystery, but I speak concerning Christ and the church" (Eph. 5:32).

How came the Church into existence? By a beating process; for the Lamb was that block of gold. God Himself worked upon Him, for Isaiah says: "It pleased the Lord to bruise Him" (53:10a). And what a bruising it was! In His birth He was unrecognized, unwanted; it was marred by poverty, no home, no bed. In His life He was despised, misjudged, misunderstood. He knew hunger and thirst, weariness of body and anguish of soul. He was robbed of reputation; His works were marred by man's unbelief. Then came Gethsemane and Calvary with the physical exhaustion, the lash, the nails, the sword, the crown of thorns, the mocking reed, the smiting, the spitting. Oh, the tragedy and the travesty!

Yet through it all, His birth was a wonderful birth, His works were mighty works; His character was a holy character; His life was a perfect life; His body was a glorious body; His death was a triumphant death; His resurrection was a firstfruits resurrection. And it was all consummated by His ascending up on high, there to make intercession for us—but not before He had promised to send a Helper, the Holy Spirit. With the descent of the Holy Spirit there came into being that glorious body of believers called the Church which, through the ages, has ever been increasing and bearing its light and testimony, and will do so until the day when He presents it—a glorious body—before His Father with exceeding joy.

This union of the believer with Christ is exhibited throughout Scripture. Eve was formed out of the side of Adam, and was "bone of his bone." Therefore the two shall be one. Christ said, "I am the vine, you are the branches" (John 15:5a). "As the branch cannot bear fruit of itself, unless it abides in the vine, neither can you, unless you abide in Me" (John 15:4b). In the lampstand we have the same metaphor, the main shaft being typical of Christ and the branches of the believers.

Christ the Shaft. The Hebrew word here translated "shaft" is *yarek* and means "thigh." Twenty times the word is translated "thigh," twice "loins," four times "side," and once "body." Genesis 46:26, Exodus 1:5, and Judges 8:30 show that *yarek is* connected with birth: "the persons who came out of the loins of Jacob," etc. What a matchless picture! Christ the *yarek,* we proceeding from Him and yet of Him. "In Him we live and move and have our being . . ." (Acts 17:28). A branch of the menorah broken off from the shaft would be a useless thing. Being curved and having no base, such a branch would not stand upright and, therefore, could not hold a lamp. So are *we* apart from Christ. We are entirely dependent upon Him!

We the Branches. It is not easy to ascertain the actual shape of the branches, but what is to be noticed is that there are seven branches. The base and its shaft constitute the central branch; then there are six more branches, three out of either side. Moreover, the central "branch" has bowls and ornamental knobs and flowers, four of each, while the six branches have three bowls each but only one knob and one flower. Pictures and diagrams that have appeared in books and other tabernacle illustrations have rarely revealed this design because they are usually only artists' impressions.

Do not think that we are too particular over the detail. In reality, we have not been particular enough, because the Lord God repeated several times to Moses: "See to it that you make it according to the pattern." This emphasis is made because there is purpose in the pattern. The Lord would now say to us: "See to it that you study and understand it according to the pattern." Gazing upon its form, lessons stand out clearly. The shaft, including the base—like the vine with its roots—is typical of Christ in His eternal and divine person—from whom all believers emerge and upon whom the whole Church stands.

Scripture speaks of the Messiah Himself as "the Branch" (Zech. 3:8, 6:12). Six branches come out of the lampstand's sides; so we conclude that the *central* branch comes out of the top of the shaft as a continuation—in which case this branch obviously stands preeminently high above the other branches. To see it thus is in perfect accord with Scripture because in this branch one can see the eternal Christ in His humanity made like His creaturely brothers and as one who is not ashamed to call *us* brothers, as we read in Hebrews 2. But also it is said of Christ: "Therefore God, Your God, has anointed You with the oil of gladness more than Your companions" (Heb. 1:9b).

Six branches come from the sides, none from the front, because the believer must stand aside to give preeminence and glory to the eternal Christ. Six is the symbolical number of man—he who was created on the sixth day in the likeness of God but who has come short of divine perfection. These six branches portray man *redeemed*; and in the midst of these branches, yet *above* them, is the seventh branch—the Perfect Man, the Man Christ Jesus.

What an amount is said concerning . . .

The Design. The pattern of the six branches differs from the seventh in detail but not in principle, because in them all there are bowls, ornamental knobs, and flowers.

The Knobs will come under our consideration first, because these are to be found also on the shaft; there are three of them, one under each pair of branches. Great difference of opinion exists as to the actual appearance of the bowls, knobs, and flowers. Therefore, we can only weigh the evidence we have and draw a conclusion. Both Josephus and rabbinic writers say that the knob was a pomegranate, some suggesting it to be the bud and others the fruit; but, as the Vulgate and the Septuagint render it "ball" or "knob," we will harmonize all by accepting it as the *fruit* of the pomegranate, which is roughly a ball in shape and is seen in much Eastern ornamentation.

In any case, the pomegranate is an emblem of peace, and is seen on the hem of the high priest's garments, in the adornment of Solomon's Temple, and in the beautiful garden of love in the Song of Solomon. A round ball is a token of completeness or perfection. Thus, from the whole evidence, we can see "peace, perfect peace." Three (the symbolical number of divinity) knobs on the main shaft—indicates God's eternal peace. Four (the symbolical number of earth) knobs on the central branch—shows forth Christ's earthly peace. Manifested when? (1) At the time of His birth, peace was announced: "Glory to God in the highest, and on earth peace . . ." (Luke 2:14). (2) In His ministry, He labored "to guide our feet into the way of peace" (Luke 1:79b). (3) In His death, He "made peace through the blood of His cross . . ." (Col. 1:20). (4) And issuing from His resurrection: "Now may the God of peace, who brought up our Lord Jesus from the dead . . ." (Heb. 13:20). In addition, on each of the six *branches* there is one knob, thus teaching us that God's peace is *our* peace. The apostle says: "Now may the Lord of peace Himself give you peace always in every way . . ." (2 Thess. 3:16).

The Bowls. The Hebrew word translated "bowls" here is *gebiya*. The word is also translated "cup" in Genesis 44:2, 12, 16 and 17, and "pot" in Jeremiah 35:5 (A.V.). It occurs nowhere else. Although the Authorized Version likens these bowls to "almonds," most later translations say "shaped like almond blossoms." *Young's Literal Translation* calls them "calyxes." "Calyx" is a botanical term in use today and signifies a cup-shaped organ or cavity, such as the outer covering or leaflike envelope of a flower. The principal function of the calyx is to enclose and protect the other parts of the flower while in bud. The calyx frequently plays a part in connection with fruit dispersal. From this we conclude that calyxes of the almond flower were included in the design of the menorah. Our hearts are gripped by the truth that, as the calyx protects the bud of new life and also the seed of next year's life, and in many cases is the progenitor of life, so Christ Himself protects and is the source of all life. "In Him was life; and the life was the light of men" (John 1:4). In Him is the bud of human life and the seed of eternal life—for the whole world is represented in the *four* "bowls."

As not every seed in the botanical world germinates, so not every possessor of human life believes unto eternal life. Three calyxes were in each of the branches, reminding us that we have received the life of the Father and of the Son and of the Holy Spirit, and that we can impart the blessings of that life to others and so help to enlarge the Church of God because "now all things are of God, who has reconciled us to Himself through Jesus Christ, and has given us the ministry of reconciliation" (2 Cor. 5:18).

The Flowers. These are accepted to be lilies, and the lily of Palestine is the wild anemone—such as Solomon in all the glory of his array could not be likened unto. Lilies along with pomegranates adorned the pillars of the temple, and the same word "flower" (*tsiyts*) is used in connection with the golden crown of the high priest. Although a fading flower, it is a picture of beauty. Four flowers on the central branch tell of the inconceivable and unsurpassable beauty of the Man of Galilee. He showed the beauty of holiness. He exhibited beauty of character in His life on earth. While there were four flowers in the central branch, there was only one in each of the other six. Did not the psalmist pray: "Let the beauty of the Lord our God be upon us"? The only beauty of which the Christian has to boast is the beauty of

Christian character. It is through us that the world sees Jesus. Christlike character will always attract. As these flowers were the crowning design of each branch, into these flowers would be set the burning lamps of testimony. For what purpose were . . .

The Lamps. Without the lamps the rest would be mere ornamentation. Beauty must be linked with usefulness. The purpose of the Church is to radiate light. It must be noticed that the light of the menorah illuminated the tabernacle, for it was in the Holy Place and not outside. We should be very concerned about our life in the Church—our witness before God and our fellow believers—because, if that is right, it must of necessity be right in the world outside.

There are, however, many professors in the Church who have a form of godliness but deny the power thereof. Of course, it was not the lamp that made the light, it only bore it. The light originated from the pure oil that was constantly being put within the lamp. Was not Pentecost the pouring in of the oil of the Holy Spirit, making the Church—now formed by the sufferings and death of Christ which had just taken place—a bold, bright Church? This same Holy Spirit had been previously given to the Lamp of the central branch when He was baptized by John in the Jordan River and the Dove descended upon Him. Jesus said, "I am the light of the world . . ." (John 8:12). "Let your light so shine before men, that they may see your good works and glorify your Father in heaven" (Matt. 5:16).

Reference has been made to the fact that it shone

inside the tabernacle, not outside. To this end was it
created. "And he lit the lamps *before the Lord* . . ."
(Ex. 40:25). The Church of Jesus Christ should ever
remember that she lives before the Lord and she labors before the Lord. Singleness of eye and purity of
motive must, therefore, be the incentive of all we
do. Moses did not light the lamps before the *world*,
but the world did know the lamps were alight. May
we ever seek to live only for Christ's glory, and the
world will say: "These people have been with Jesus
and learned from Him."

We are also informed that the lampstand stood
opposite the table of showbread (Ex. 26:35). Through
the light of the Spirit manifested in the Church comes
true knowledge and the provision for glowing fellowship—as we feast *with* Him and *on* Him, the true
Bread that came down from heaven.

The lampstand also sent a beam of light onto the
golden altar and the veil before which that altar of
incense stood. So it illuminated the place of intercession. Shall we not, in the Spirit, lift our hearts in
prayer for the final rending of that veil, saying: "Even
so, come, Lord Jesus"?

Finally, "the lamps gave light in front of" the
lampstand itself. If the Church shines before the Lord,
it will unconsciously shine upon itself. Moses' face
shone though he knew it not. He had been in the
presence of God. Stephen looked steadfastly into
heaven and his face was as the face of an angel.

Two small, but indispensable, things accompanied
the lampstand. They were the . . .

Wick-trimmers and the Trays. The lamps would

need to be trimmed; in fact, they were trimmed every morning and evening. During their hours of burning, the wicks would burn low and the trimmers would be needed to lift them up. Then too, soot would sometimes accumulate on a wick, causing the light to burn dimly. This soot was not caused by the oil—for it was pure—but by the consumption of the wick itself. So the trimmers were needed to nip off the soot, and the trays to carry it away.

How often do things come into our lives that hinder our testimony and cause the flame of devotion to burn low. Then the Lord comes with His trimmers of reproof or chastisement to remove that hindrance: "For whom the Father loves He chastens." We often blame the Enemy for attacks which are possibly the trimmers of the Lord seeking to refine us so that we may bear a better light. Let us allow the Lord to do what He desires for our good, or He may say: "Repent, or I will remove your lampstand from its place." The Lord may remove the lamp from the place of service, but we can rejoice in that He does not carry an extinguisher to put the light out.

CHAPTER 13

The Table of Showbread

Exodus 25:23–30; 31:8; 37:10–16. Leviticus 24:5–9.
Hebrews 9:2.

"You shall also make a table of acacia wood; two cubits shall be its length, a cubit its width, and a cubit and a half its height. And you shall overlay it with pure gold, and make a molding of gold all around. You shall make for it a frame of a handbreadth all around, and you shall make a gold molding for the frame all around. And you shall make for it four rings of gold, and put the rings on the four corners that are at its four legs. The rings shall be close to the frame, as holders for the poles to bear the table. And you shall make the poles of acacia wood, and overlay them with gold, that the table may be carried with them. You shall make its dishes, its pans, its pitchers, and its bowls for pouring. You shall make them of pure gold. And you shall set the showbread on the table before Me always." (Ex. 25:23–30)

"And you shall take fine flour and bake twelve cakes with it. Two-tenths of an ephah shall be in each cake. You shall set them in two rows, six in a row, on the pure table before the Lord. And you shall put pure frankincense on each row, that it may be on the bread for a memorial, an offering made by fire to the Lord. Every Sabbath he shall set it in order before the Lord continually, being taken from the children of Israel by an ever-lasting covenant. And it shall be for Aaron and his sons, and they shall eat it in a holy place; for it is most holy to him from the offerings of the Lord made by fire, by a perpetual statute." (Lev. 24:5–9)

OPPOSITE the lampstand, on the north side of the Holy Place, stood the table of showbread with its twelve loaves. There is something charming and appealing about this piece of furniture. It speaks of fellowship; it is an emblem of friendship. When we desire to have fellowship with an acquaintance whom we may casually meet in town, we say: "Come and have a cup of coffee." If we desire to know our friend even more intimately—wanting to tell him things and to learn more about him—it is customary to ask him home for a meal. How precious! The Lord of Glory similarly desires fellowship with His redeemed ones! He desires more than casual acquaintance—that is, that we should know Him better. He has therefore provided a table. David said: "You prepare a table before me in the presence of my enemies." This table points to the one provided in the tabernacle for priests only. How plainly it speaks of the Lord's Table around which saints gather from week to week. We call it the Communion, or the Breaking of Bread. Do we know communion? The word means "fellowship."

But let us come back to the table in the tabernacle.

Its Size was two by one by one-and-a-half cubits. That is, the same height as the ark of the covenant but half a cubit less in length and breadth; but when the handbreadth frame, or rim, with its gold molding is added, it is brought roughly to the same size. Measurements imply limitations. The table is large enough to receive all who are worthy to come—which is the whole priesthood—but small enough to exclude all who are not worthy. Judas, having partaken of the first meal, was exposed and took his leave before the institution of the Last Supper. No traitor should be at the Table of the Lord, nor yet any unbeliever. That is why the apostle said: "But let a man examine *himself*, and so let him eat of that bread and drink of that cup. For he who eats and drinks in an unworthy manner eats and drinks judgment to himself, not discerning the Lord's body" (1 Cor. 11:28–29).

The Materials of this table correspond with those of the remaining furniture—acacia wood overlaid with gold. As acacia wood is that which tells of the humanity of Christ while gold speaks of His divinity, so would we call to mind a twofold fellowship which Holy Writ shows to be ours. First, the wood of Christ's human life and His sojourning among men. What do we know of it? Paul says: "That I may know Him and the power of His resurrection, and the fellowship of His sufferings, being conformed to His death" (Phil. 3:10). Identification with His death means recognition in His glory, which is the gold of the table. Paul writing again says: ". . . that you may be blameless in the day of our Lord Jesus Christ. God is faithful, by whom you were called into the fellowship of His Son, Jesus Christ our Lord" (1 Cor.

1:8–9) and "If we endure, we shall also reign with Him . . ." (2 Tim. 2:12).

The table, as far as we have looked at it, was quite ordinary, but there were some features that made it extraordinary. It had a frame, two moldings, rings and carrying-poles, all of which are very interesting to the child of God.

The Frame, which was a handbreadth in width— about four and a half inches—appears to be an addition to the table area. It is difficult to ascertain from the text as to whether this was on the same level as the table surface or lower, as some suggest. The relief on the Arch of Titus—which is often referred to as a guide to this table and the menorah—is no guide or help at all because that arch commemorates the destruction of the Herod's Temple and the carrying away of *its* furniture, and we know that the style of some of the furniture in the temple was quite different from that of the tabernacle. One thing is certain about this encircling frame: it was extra to the table. Seeing that the lesser measurements are those of the table and that a table is not a table without legs, this frame, as an addition, must have overhung the legs. The reason we seek to emphasize this is because the twelve loaves rested upon the table while, possibly, the frame with its molding served as a place for the vessels of the table, namely the dishes, pans, pitchers, and bowls. The bread, therefore—typical of the Word of God—rested upon the sound foundation of the four legs while the utensils had no foundation at all.

Believer, do you not see that our only sure

authority, our only certainty, our only spiritual food, is the Word of God? Christ declared, "Heaven and earth will pass away, but My words will by no means pass away" (Matt. 24:35). This Word becomes the food of the Christian. By it he is built up in his faith. The vessels, we have noted, found their place in the extended border. They were ordained by God and were used in connection with the table and the bread; but they were not food and could not be eaten. Could not we liken these utensils to all manner of Bible helps—commentaries, concordances, studies, ministries, books (including this one)? While many of them are blessed by God, they are only to help us in our understanding of God's Word. We must not take these things as authoritative. They lack the foundation of divine inspiration and are not God-breathed. There is a great need today to call men back to the Book as the final authority.

The second distinctive was . . .

The Moldings. There were two of them, one for the table and one for the frame. These decorations may have had the general appearance of "crowns," and that is the way the translators of the Authorized Version understood the Hebrew *zer*. Their purpose appears to have been to keep things in their respective places. The first kept the bread on the table; the second prevented things from falling off the frame. God has ever preserved His Word thus by the Holy Spirit. Some people would confuse things and mix the divine and the human elements, accepting man's word to be as authoritative as the Bible, but God holds the Book aloft as His. There are yet others who would push ministries and everything else of a spiritual nature to the background, but again the crown of God's Holy Spirit protects all who are, and all that is, sanctified by the Spirit. To change the type: the twice-crowned table of wood and gold reminds us of the twice-crowned Lord who provided for us the Bread of Life. In the wood of His humanity He was crowned with thorns by wicked men. In the gold of His divine life God has eternally crowned Him with glory and honor.

The third feature of this table that distinguishes it from other tables was that it had . . .

Rings and Poles, their purposes being, of course, to bear the table. Tables usually have a permanent position. While this table had its place and position, yet it was adapted to its wilderness journeys. The people at this time were pilgrims. They traveled and the table traveled with them. Here is a blessed thought: God has given to us spiritual food, not in the form of a church or a ministry but in written words, in a book. We can carry it in our pocket or in a handbag. We can put it in our case when we travel, by our bedside when we retire at night. I have read my Bible on the top of mountains in solitude, on the bus amid the crowds of London, in the subway rushing through the bosom of the earth, in the hospital in the hour of sickness, as well as in the church in the hour of worship. I have found the opportunity for meditation at home in the morning, at noon, at night, yea, anytime and anywhere—adaptability.

With regard to the . . .

Vessels, suffice it to say that, so far as evidence

shows, the *dishes or chargers* were used for the conveying of the bread to the table. The *pans* or *spoons* undoubtedly were used for putting the incense onto the bread and possibly for carrying incense to the golden altar. Twelve gold pans were given by the princes according to Numbers 7; see verse 14, and every sixth verse onward. The summary is in verse 86: "The twelve gold pans full of incense weighed ten shekels apiece, according to the shekel of the sanctuary; all the gold of the pans weighed one hundred and twenty shekels."

Pitchers and *bowls* are the last two items mentioned which, according to the Vulgate, Septuagint, Syriac, and most other authorities, were "flagons" and "chalices." These vessels were used in connection with the drink offering that always accompanied the meal offering. Some of the drink offerings were poured out at the bronze altar and some in the Holy Place. "And its drink offering shall be one-fourth of a hin for each lamb; in a holy place you shall pour out the drink to the Lord as an offering" (Num. 28:7). Those poured out in the Holy Place were not poured out at the golden altar, however, because "You shall not offer strange incense on it, or a burnt offering, or a meal offering; nor shall you pour a drink offering on it" (Ex. 30:9). The evidence then is that it was poured out before the table of showbread where, we understand, the wine was with the bread.

So much for the table, but we must spend a little time on the most important thing, although reference already has been made to it. It was not the bronze altar but the sacrifice thereon that atoned. It was not the laver but the water therein that cleansed. Neither was it the lampstand but the light thereof that illuminated, nor the golden altar but the incense that sanctified. Likewise with the ark of the covenant, the blood-sprinkled mercy seat was the propitiation. Here at the table . . .

The Showbread was that upon which the priests fed. The full details concerning this bread are found in Leviticus 24:5–9. Reference has been made to the fact that the bread is a type of the Word of God, that is, Christ the Written Word. But Christ is also the Living Word. The loaves were to be made of fine flour; nothing coarse or inferior would ever suffice in those things that pointed to the Perfect One. The flour, a product of the earth, had not only to be ground in the mill but sieved, tested, and proved to be "fine" flour before it could be used for showbread, or "presence-bread," or the "bread of faces" as it is sometimes called. This is a picture of the Living Word. He not only passed through the mill of suffering, but also was tested and proved as "fine" and perfect in character. Here is the verdict:

Pilate said, "I find no fault in this man" (Luke 23:4).

Pilate's wife said, "Have nothing to do with that just man" (Matt. 27:19).

Judas said, "I have sinned by betraying innocent blood" (Matt. 27:4).

The criminal said, "This man has done nothing wrong" (Luke 23:41).

The centurion said, "Certainly this was a righteous man" (Luke 23:47).

God said, "My beloved Son, in whom I am well pleased" (Matt. 17:5).

He was indeed "holy, harmless, undefiled, separate from sinners" (Heb. 7:26).

It matters not how fine the quality of the flour; by itself it cannot be eaten. It is, therefore, necessary to bake it. In the case of the unleavened showbread it was baked in a fierce or quick oven. Was it not so with Christ? While His character was flawless and His life perfect, that could not meet the needs of failing man or satisfy the demands of a holy God. Christ, therefore, was pierced with holes all over—like *matzah*—and then He passed through the fierce oven of Calvary and came out the Bread of Life, the Satisfier of those who trust Him.

There were twelve cakes perpetually laid on the table. They were eaten by the priests each week. Those priests, however many in number, were the representatives of God to the people and of the people to God. Therefore, as they feasted upon the unleavened bread, representatively all twelve tribes feasted. God in Christ can and does provide for the whole Church.

Why did God tell them to put frankincense upon the cakes? We think of the spiritual application of purity, but as to actual and practical use we do not know. Did it sweeten the bread? We *do* know that Christ as the Bread of Life is not dry and uninteresting, but, rather, sweet to our taste, yea, sweeter than honey! Before the priests partook of the cakes, other cakes were put in their place; thus there was never any lack. No one has ever come to the table of the

Lord to find no food awaiting.

CHAPTER 14

The Altar of Incense

Exodus 30:1–10; 37:25–29; 30:34–38.

"You shall make an altar to burn incense on; you shall make it of acacia wood. A cubit shall be its length and a cubit its width—it shall be square—and two cubits shall be its height. Its horns shall be of one piece with it. And you shall overlay its top, its sides all around, and its horns with pure gold; and you shall make for it a molding of gold all around. Two gold rings you shall make for it, under the molding on both its sides. You shall place them on its two sides, and they will be holders for the poles with which to bear it. You shall make the poles of acacia wood, and overlay them with gold. And you shall put it before the veil that is before the ark of the Testimony, before the mercy seat that is over the Testimony, where I will meet with you. Aaron shall burn on it sweet incense every morning; when he tends the lamps, he shall burn incense on it. And when Aaron lights the lamps at twilight, he shall burn incense on it, a perpetual incense before the Lord throughout your generations. You shall not offer strange incense on it, or a burnt offering, or a meal offering; nor shall you pour a drink offering on it. And Aaron shall make atonement upon its horns once a year with the blood of the sin offering of atonement; once a year he shall make atonement upon it throughout your generations. It is most holy to the Lord." (Ex: 30:1–10)

And the Lord said to Moses: "Take sweet spices, stacte, and onycha and galbanum, and pure frankincense with these sweet spices; there shall be equal amounts of each. You shall make of these an incense, a compound according to the art of the perfumer, salted, pure, and holy. And you shall beat some of it very fine, and put some of it before the Testimony in the tabernacle of meeting where I will meet with you. It shall be most holy to you. But as for the incense which you shall make, you shall not make any for yourselves, according to its composition. It shall be to you holy for the Lord. Whoever makes any like it, to smell it, he shall be cut off from his people." (Ex. 30:34–38)

THE ALTAR of incense stood directly in line with the center of the entrance to the tabernacle and further inside than the other two pieces of furniture. We are informed that its position was "before the veil." It was only a small piece of furniture, standing two cubits high and one cubit broad and long, or three feet six inches high and about twenty-one inches square. It was just large enough to serve its purpose.

There does not appear to be anything significant in its measurements—we must not force the type just to make something out of it. True, it is higher than the table and the mercy seat, but it is in good proportion. One noticeable thing is that it is definitely the smallest piece of furniture. That would not justify us in saying that it was less important than the rest, because that would be untrue. Neither is it good reasoning to speak of its being higher in importance. There is a peculiar interweaving of truth that binds each piece within (or to) the other and makes them all indispensable, none being more important than the others because all are essential. Might not the smallness of this representation of intercession remind one that it is not the length or the size of the prayer that prevails, but its reality? Did not the Lord say that we were not heard for our many words, for our vain repetitions? Fervent, righteous prayer avails much.

The Materials were again twofold: wood and gold. Thus the *man Christ Jesus* makes intercession in *heaven* for the believing Church on *earth*.

A Molding or Crown kept the fire from falling to the ground. When the incense was brought by the priest, the fire was there to cause that incense to rise to God. Fire is one of the many descriptions used for the Holy Spirit. The Apostle Paul says: "The Spirit Himself makes intercession for us . . ." (Rom. 8:26b). The prayers of Christ never fail. Peter stumbled, but just before that the Lord had said to Peter, "Simon, Simon! Indeed, Satan has asked for you, that he may sift you as wheat. But I have prayed for you . . ." (Luke 22:31–32).

Horns were also to be found on this altar. Here they tell of the power of prayer, prayer that can reach to the four corners of the earth. Abram interceded for Sodom and prevailed as long as he prayed. Jacob wrestled all night at Peniel and became Israel. Ezekiel pleaded for Jerusalem. We need to lay hold of the horns of prevailing prayer.

Rings and Poles adapted the altar to wilderness experiences as they did the table of showbread. Christ was ever in the midst of His people to hear their cry, and He still is. To the woman of Samaria He said: "Woman, believe Me, the hour is coming when you will neither on this mountain, nor in Jerusalem, worship the Father. . . . But the hour is coming, and now is, when the true worshipers will worship the Father in spirit and truth; for the Father is seeking such to worship Him" (John 4:21–23). Intercession is limited to neither time nor place.

Its Purpose. The altar shows forth the greater work of Christ, who has already accomplished a great work. Having finished the work of redemption for the world, He went up on high to become the great Mediator between God and man, and the great Intercessor hearing our cry and pleading our cause. We, as the sons of the great High Priest, have received the same high calling in Christ Jesus.

Its position was in the direct line of approach to the mercy seat, therefore, before the ark of the covenant. The ark was the dwelling place of God, He saying: "There I will meet with you, and I will speak with you from above the mercy seat, from between the two cherubim which are on the ark of the Testimony . . ." (Ex. 25:22a). The altar of incense holds the same position in heaven as it did on earth, as can be seen in Revelation 8:3: "Then another angel, having a golden censer, came and stood at the altar. And he was given much incense, that he should offer it with the prayers of all the saints upon the golden altar which was before the throne." The only difference between the two is that once there hung a veil between, but now there is no veil, seeing it has been rent in two. And we have boldness to enter into His presence.

There appears to be a special relationship between the three pieces of furniture in the Holy Place, created by the ministry of the priests between the one and the other. The principal link was between the lampstand and the altar. Verses 7 and 8 of Exodus 30 tell how the priest put incense on the golden altar at the time of the trimming of the lamps, both morning and evening. These were joint ministries. They always will be, prayer and testimony going together. It has been wisely said: "We shine best before men [the lampstand] when our hearts burn most before God [the altar]." This connection is readily seen throughout Scripture. Isaiah 6:5–9: "Then I said, 'Woe is me, for I am undone! Because I am a man of unclean lips, and I dwell in the midst of a people of unclean lips; for my eyes have seen the King, the Lord of hosts.' Then one of the seraphim flew to me, having in his hand a live coal which he had taken with the tongs from the altar. And he touched my mouth with it, and said: 'Behold, this has touched your lips; your iniquity is taken away, and your sin purged.' Also I heard the voice of the Lord, saying: 'Whom shall I send, and who will go for Us?' Then I said, 'Here am I! Send me.' And He said, 'Go. . . .'" Isaiah received a touch from the golden altar with his commission to "go" and minister. "I will put My Spirit within you . . ." (the altar); "Then the nations which are left all around you shall know . . ." (the lampstand) (Ezek. 36:27, 36). "But you shall receive power when the Holy Spirit has come upon you [the altar]; and you shall be witnesses to Me in Jerusalem, and in all Judea and Samaria, and to the end of the earth [the lampstand]" (Acts 1:8).

I have sometimes thought of this little piece of furniture standing before the veil as an electric plug such as we use to tap the electric power from the wires laid behind our walls. Behind the veil of the tabernacle was the *Shekinah* glory of the presence of the Lord, and behind the veil of the sky are all the resources of the great triune Godhead. By putting in the plug of prayer with the hand of faith, we are able to tap those resources and find that "prayer changes things."

Great things happen at the hour of prayer when incense is being offered. "And it came to pass, at the time of the offering of the evening sacrifice, that Elijah the prophet came near and said, 'Lord God of Abraham, Isaac, and Israel, let it be known this day that You are God in Israel. . . .' Then the fire of the Lord fell . . ." (1 Kings 18:36, 38). "Yes, while I was speaking in prayer, the man Gabriel, whom I had seen in the vision at the beginning, being caused to fly swiftly, reached me about the time of the evening offering" (Dan. 9:21). Then it was that Daniel received a revelation concerning the future of his people. "Now Peter and John went up together to the temple at the hour of prayer, the *ninth hour*" (Acts 3:1). In their going they met and healed the lame man at the beautiful gate. "And Cornelius said, 'Four days ago I was fasting until this hour; and at the *ninth hour* I prayed in my house, and behold, a man stood before me in bright clothing, and said, "Cornelius, your prayer has been heard . . .""" (Acts 10:30–31). The result was that the gospel went to the Gentiles. "Now from the sixth hour until the ninth hour there was darkness over all the land. And about the *ninth hour* Jesus cried with a loud voice. . . . Jesus, when He had cried out again with a loud voice, yielded up His spirit. And behold, the veil of the temple was torn in two . . ." (Matt. 27:45–51).

The right use of the place of prayer brings much blessing, while the abuse of it brings a curse: "So Azariah the priest went in after him, and with him were eighty priests of the Lord, who were valiant men. And they withstood King Uzziah, and said to him, 'It is not for you, Uzziah, to burn incense to the Lord, but for the priests, the sons of Aaron, who are consecrated to burn incense. Get out of the sanctuary, for you have trespassed! You shall have no honor from the Lord God.' Then Uzziah became furious; and he had a censer in his hand to burn incense. And while he was angry with the priests, leprosy broke out on his forehead, before the priests in the house of the Lord, beside the incense altar" (2 Chron. 26:17–19).

Before passing on to the incense, there is quite a contrast between the two altars which ought to be observed. The bronze altar was outside and the golden altar inside. The outside altar was made of wood and was strengthened with bronze; the inside altar was likewise made of wood, but it was beautified with gold. The first altar had no crown—Christ in His humiliation. The second had a crown—Christ in His exaltation. The bronze altar was the place of suffering and typifies Christ as Savior. The golden altar was the place of triumph and typifies Christ as the Mediator. To the first came the sinner; the second was for the saint.

Beside contrast there is also similarity. Both altars were square, symmetrical—a sign of solidity and equality. At the one is seen Christ dying for the whole world, irrespective of color or race; at the other Christ is seen interceding for the whole Church of believers, irrespective of denomination or creed, providing they are "born again." Both have the rings and poles of non-isolation, and both have the symbol of universal strength—four horns.

The Incense. As was stated in the last chapter, the value of the altar was in the incense. This was a mysterious compound carefully made with equal proportions of stacte, onycha, galbanum and frankincense. Someone has beautifully typified this wonderful confection of equality with the great work of Christ as: (1) The merit of His life; (2) The merit of His death; (3) The merit of His resurrection; to which is added: (4) the frankincense of His ascension. Which was the most important of these? None! for they are inseparable. His perfect life could not redeem, so His death was necessary. His death would not have been efficacious if His life had not been sinless, therefore, these are equal. Yet it needed His resurrection to show us that God was satisfied and had accepted the work; and, if there had been no resurrection and Christ had remained in the grave, we would have had no Intercessor, no one to present our prayers faultless before God. The resurrection, therefore, was as important as the life and death. The consummation of His lifework on earth was His ascension.

"See that you make nothing like it" was a very definite injunction given. "It shall be most holy to you . . . for the Lord." Could anything be made that would equal the compound of Christ's incarnate life? No! Then why did God give such a command? Because He knew that men would seek to make an imitation. There is but one Mediator, but man has ordained his "priests" and established his "confessions." The Bible says: "Do not call anyone on earth your father; for One is your Father, He who is in heaven" (Matt. 23:9). Yet there is an order of men in certain sections of the church who are called "Father" and officiate as priests. Surely such is contrary to the Word of God and is an abomination in His sight. There is "one Mediator between God and men, the Man Christ Jesus" (1 Tim. 2:5b). "And having a High Priest over the house of God, let us draw near with a true heart in full assurance of faith . . ." (Heb. 10:21–22).

Chapter 15

The Veil

Exodus 26:31–37. Mark 15:38. Hebrews 9 and 10.

"You shall make a veil woven of blue and purple and scarlet yarn, and fine linen thread. It shall be woven with an artistic design of cherubim. You shall hang it upon the four pillars of acacia wood overlaid with gold. Their hooks shall be of gold, upon four sockets of silver. And you shall hang the veil from the clasps. Then you shall bring the ark of the Testimony in there, behind the veil. The veil shall be a divider for you between the holy place and the Most Holy. You shall put the mercy seat upon the ark of the Testimony in the Most Holy. You shall set the table outside the veil, and the lampstand across from the table on the side of the tabernacle toward the south; and you shall put the table on the north side. You shall make a screen for the door of the tabernacle, woven of blue and purple and scarlet yarn, and fine linen thread, made by a weaver. And you shall make for the screen five pillars of acacia wood, and overlay them with gold; their hooks shall be of gold, and you shall cast five sockets of bronze for them." (Ex. 26:31–37)

Then the veil of the temple was torn in two from top to bottom. (Mk. 15:38)

SIX different veils are spoken of in Scripture. They are:

1. The Veil of the Tabernacle. Which is our study.

2. The Veil of the Temple. "And he made the veil of blue and purple and crimson and fine linen, and wove cherubim into it" (2 Chron. 3:14). This was not the same veil as was in the tabernacle. Moses made the first; Solomon made the second. The veil of the tabernacle would have been useless in the massive temple, the measurements being extreme.

3. The Veil of Moses. "And when Moses had finished speaking with them, he put a veil on his face. But whenever Moses went in before the Lord to speak with Him, he would take the veil off until he came out; and he would come out and speak to the children of Israel whatever he had been commanded. And whenever the children of Israel saw the face of Moses, that the skin of Moses' face shone, then Moses would put the veil on his face again, until he went in to speak with Him" (Ex. 34:33–35). The glorious character of the Godhead had secretly stamped itself upon Moses' face. The veil was necessary to conceal the glory from the mortal eyes of man.

4. The Veil of Christ's Flesh. "Therefore, brethren, having boldness to enter the Holiest by the blood of Jesus, by a new and living way which He consecrated for us, through the veil, that is, His flesh . . ." (Heb. 10:19–20). The human frame that Christ took upon Himself was a veil which hid the inner glory of the divine life. Once in His life on the earth that glory burst through the veil, on the Mount of Transfiguration (Matt. 17:2).

5. The Veil of Unbelief. "Unlike Moses, who put a veil over his face so that the children of Israel could not look steadily at the end of what was passing away. But their minds were hardened. For until this day . . . when Moses is read, a veil lies on their heart. Nevertheless when one turns to the Lord, the veil is taken away" (2 Cor. 3:13–16). This means that, while they read the Law, they did not discern its principles.

6. The Veil of National Blindness. "And He will destroy on this mountain the surface of the covering cast over all people, and the veil that is spread over all nations. . . . And it will be said in that day: 'Behold, this is our God; we have waited for Him, and He will save us. This is the Lord; we have waited for Him; we will be glad and rejoice in His salvation'" (Isa. 25:7–9). The veil is over the scattered people of God, but, when it is removed, they will recognize Him whom they pierced and say: "Blessed is He who comes in the name of the Lord." Then shall a nation be born in a day.

In each instance the veil is that which comes between and hides.

The veil of the tabernacle hung upon . . .

Four Pillars made of acacia wood and overlaid with gold. The reason why there were four pillars to the veil in comparison with five to the door is obvious when we realize that the space was less, as the five pillars were undoubtedly on the front of the tabernacle, and the outer pillars overlapped the edge of the first boards. While the five pillars of the door remind us of grace and their golden capitals speak of the sovereign grace that brought us access, the four pillars inside tell us of the solidity of the work, as do the altars with their four equal sides. The foundation of these pillars consisted of . . .

Silver Sockets. Redemption is not only the ground upon which the believer stands but is also the foundation and eternal purpose of Christ's cross work.

The Gold Hooks above both the veil and the door remind us of the fact that the divine hand of God was ever upon His Son, upholding Him, and sustaining Him in all His earthly life.

The outstanding feature of the four pillars of the veil was that they lacked an architectural finish. Columns are usually finished with a capital. This you can see in all public buildings, in the Temple of Solomon, and on all the pillars of the tabernacle with the exception of these four. No capital is mentioned at all. Is this an omission on the part of the writer? I think not, seeing that he was guided by divine inspiration. These pillars, upholding the veil that was to be rent, have a link with it, which has been expressed by the late Henry Soltau in the following words:

> May not our thoughts be directed by this to the contemplation of those scriptures which speak of the Lord as cut off? Isaiah 53:8: "Who shall declare his generation? for he was cut off out of the land of the living." And Psalm 102:23–24: "He shortened my days. I said, O my God, take me not

away in the midst of my days!" And yet the very fact of this seemingly abrupt termination of the life of the Lord Jesus, in the days of His flesh, has made Him to be unto us "wisdom, righteousness, sanctification, and redemption": a fourfold perfection meeting our fourfold need, to which possibly the number of veil pillars may allude.

The Veil. We learn from Hebrews 10:20 that the veil refers to Christ's flesh, His life upon earth. This was the "Word" made flesh and dwelling among us, going about and doing ceaseless good; but that was not the fullest manifestation of the love of God. We are told that the way into the immediate presence of God was not made manifest while the veil remained unrent. So then, the veil is His life, and the rending of the veil His death. His death, of course, was the fullest revelation of divine love.

The character of the incarnate Son of God is manifested in the wonderful colors of the veil. We must refer the reader back to the notes in Chapter 7 about those colors in the curtains of the tabernacle. It was to be skillfully woven with . . .

Artistic Designs, the work of an artisan. We read that Bezaleel was anointed with the Spirit of God for all manner of workmanship, so the work was undoubtedly artistic, not crude. Tradition says that the veil was a handbreadth in thickness. Whether or not this is so, it was a wonderful fabric made according to a divine pattern. But no loom of earth could have made the *other* veil—"that is, His flesh." But the same Spirit who anointed Bezaleel anointed also the Virgin Mary for her special work of bringing into the world that human frame which was to embody the incarnate Godhead: "The Holy Spirit will come upon you, and the power of the Highest will overshadow you; therefore, also, that Holy One who is to be born will be called the Son of God" (Luke 1:35). "She was found with child of the Holy Spirit" (Matt. 1:18). Born of a woman and yet called the Son of God (blue). Called the Son of Man (red). Called Immanuel—"God with us" (purple).

Upon this veil were skillfully wrought figures of cherubim, the emblems of guardianship. For while this veil was wonderfully designed and beautifully attractive, yet its purpose was to keep out. It told man that he could not approach God. Christ in His ministry showed this. The apostle said in Hebrews 9:8 that as long as the first tabernacle was standing (dispensationally) the way into the Holiest was not made manifest. Even so, while Christ lived there was no redemption. But He died and, in so doing, not only opened a new and living way, but also brought the tabernacle dispensation to an end. And so we now see a . . .

Veil Rent. "And, behold, the veil of the temple was torn in two from top to bottom . . ." (Matt. 27:51). Simultaneous with the death of Christ on Calvary came this divine rending of the veil of the temple. So the way was opened—not to a mercy seat and an ark, for no ark existed in Herod's Temple. All trace of the ark had been lost hundreds of years earlier at the time when Solomon's Temple was destroyed. The death of Christ did not open the way to an ark, but to God Himself. Types are now fading away as realities shed forth their wonderful light. Christ dies to turn shadows into substance.

When referring to the veil, doctrinal passages of the New Testament include both the veil of the tabernacle and the veil of the temple for, while they were materially different, they were doctrinally the same—just as I may move into a new house and change my furniture, but it is still home, because home is not the building or the furniture but the spirit, the love, the fellowship. This veil then was . . .

1. Divinely Rent, from the top, beyond man's reach. This is true of the death of Christ. "It pleased the Lord to bruise Him." His own people rejected Him, leaders of the Jews condemned Him, Romans crucified Him, yet He said, "No one takes My life from Me, but I lay it down of Myself." With the rending of the veil came the closing of the old dispensation and the opening of a new. It was . . .

2. Rent in the Midst. The apostle said: "This thing was not done in a corner." Salvation is not something of which to be ashamed. Some people apologize for their faith. Paul said, "I am not ashamed of the gospel of Christ," and neither was God ashamed of it. It is a narrow way, a direct approach. "I am the way. . . . No one comes to the Father except through Me." It was . . .

3. Rent Completely from top to bottom, not a thread was left. I believe the veil split and parted asunder exactly as the Mount of Olives will when Christ's feet touch it (Zech. 14:4).

Unfortunately, some people show us a veil with a

rip in it, with many ragged threads of formality, ritual, law, doubt, "isms," etc., reaching from side to side, over which the sinner and the young Christian are caused to trip. But God has cleared the way and left no obstacle at all.

· CHAPTER 16 ·

The Ark of the Covenant

Exodus 25:10–22; 37:1–9.

"And they shall make an ark of acacia wood; two and a half cubits shall be its length, a cubit and a half its width, and a cubit and a half its height. And you shall overlay it with pure gold, inside and out you shall overlay it, and shall make on it a molding of gold all around. You shall cast four rings of gold for it, and put them in its four corners; two rings shall be on one side, and two rings on the other side. And you shall make poles of acacia wood, and overlay them with gold. You shall put the poles into the rings on the sides of the ark, that the ark may be carried by them. The poles shall be in the rings of the ark; they shall not be taken from it. And you shall put into the ark the Testimony which I will give you.

"You shall make a mercy seat of pure gold; two and a half cubits shall be its length and a cubit and a half its width. And you shall make two cherubim of gold; of hammered work you shall make them at the two ends of the mercy seat. Make one cherub at one end, and the other cherub at the other end; you shall make the cherubim at the two ends of it of one piece with the mercy seat. And the cherubim shall stretch out their wings above, covering the mercy seat with their wings, and they shall face one another; the faces of the cherubim shall be toward the mercy seat. You shall put the mercy seat on top of the ark, and in the ark you shall put the Testimony that I will give you. And there I will meet with you, and I will speak with you from above the mercy seat, from between the two cherubim which are on the ark of the Testimony, of all things which I will give you in commandment to the children of Israel." (Ex. 25:10–22)

WITH reverence and holy awe we step beyond the veil into the Holiest of All and gaze upon the ark of the covenant, a thing the Old Testament saints were never permitted to do. On the one day in the year when the high priest did enter, he dropped incense upon his burning censer, causing a cloud of perfumed smoke to dim his vision. As the veil is now rent, we can come with holy boldness and learn all that the ark once stood to teach us.

What Is an Ark? The dictionary says: "A chest, or coffer, for keeping safe and secret anything." Bearing this in mind, there are three, if not four, arks mentioned in the Scriptures.

Noah's Ark. "And God said to Noah . . . Make yourself an ark of gopherwood; make rooms in the ark, and cover it inside and outside with pitch" (Gen. 6:13–14). This ark kept safe and secret eight righteous persons from the judgment of God.

Moses' Ark. "But when she could no longer hide him, she took an ark of bulrushes for him, daubed it with asphalt and pitch, put the child in it, and laid it in the reeds by the river's bank" (Ex. 2:3). This ark became the salvation of one baby from the wrath of a king.

God's Ark. "And they shall make an ark of acacia wood; two and a half cubits shall be its length, a cubit and a half its width, and a cubit and a half its height" (Ex. 25:10). This chest hid the law of a holy God, because man could not keep it.

Householder's Ark. "Then he said to them, 'Therefore every scribe instructed concerning the kingdom of heaven is like a householder who brings out of his treasure [chest] things new and old'" (Matt. 13:52). It was the custom of Eastern folk to keep a chest in which they kept securely all their old heirlooms and all their new valuables. When entertaining guests, they would bring out their treasures and with pride show them to their friends. This chest was actually an ark, although not so called here.

Position. The introduction to the whole subject is really arresting. "Let them make Me a sanctuary . . . they shall make an ark." The very first detail given concerns this piece of furniture; the building itself comes later. We usually choose the furniture according to the building, but not so with the Lord. He begins where He always does, at the heart of things, working from within to without. The ark was normally the heart of the sanctuary; for a tabernacle without the ark would be like a body without a soul, or a Church without Christ. This is seen in Herod's Temple which had no true ark and was a system of religion and ritual which could do no more than crucify its Messiah.

A most detailed description is given of this piece of furniture and in every detail of it only Christ is to be seen. "They shall make an ark of . . .

Acacia Wood." This wood has a very hard, close-grained texture, and one is often reminded of the lesson of durability; but as wood is a type of humanity, there must be some deeper lesson to learn.

Acacia wood, we understand, comes from a tree that is native to the district in which the children of Israel were then sojourning and where the tabernacle was to be made. If the Lord had said, "They shall make an ark of cedar wood," it might have involved a long journey to Lebanon. If it had been oak or gopher wood, they would have had to wait until they reached Palestine; for oaks do not grow in the desert. But, no! God chose to use the wood that was common to their environment and easily accessible. Oh, the wonder of it! When God chose to incarnate Himself for man by sending His only begotten Son, He did not send Him in the form of an angel or an archangel, nor yet with a mystical body belonging to some other realm. "But He took upon Himself the form of man and was made like His brethren." Reverently we say it was just an ordinary body, knowing the same temptations, the same physical weaknesses and limitations, yet without sin. More of this phase of truth can be seen in the ark's . . .

Size. It was two and a half cubits long, and one and a half cubits high and wide. The ark then was restricted to certain measurements. Even so Christ, in the flesh, was confined to all our bodily limitations. His human strength was limited: He knew tiredness and physical exhaustion. His appetite was limited: He knew both hunger and thirst. His natural abilities were limited to the same extent as ours;

that is to say, like ourselves He could be in only one place at a time and do one thing at a time. It was not until after He had laid down the natural and had risen with a supernatural body that He was able to enter into a room with doors barred and windows locked. When our mortal shall have put on immortality, we shall be the same. How suggestive then is acacia wood; but it was all . . .

Overlaid with Gold, within and without. Gold, we have already learned, is a type of divinity. What a wonderful blending of the two natures—within the gold was wood and within the wood was gold. The outward life of Christ showed the gold of His divinity in His work, His words, His whole demeanor. His inward thoughts and motives were just as pure, just as holy. Some people's works are good, but wrong motives rob them of blessing and reward; some people mean well but act unwisely. How different the Lord was! It has been said that the gold was beaten onto the wood, and beaten so finely that the grain of the wood showed through the gold. Whether that be so or not is unrecorded in the sacred canon, and its possibility is difficult to ascertain; but we do know that, amidst all the demonstration of Christ's divinity and power, the human nature could always be seen. It was Divinity that said: "But the water that I shall give him will become in him a fountain of water springing up into everlasting life" (John 4:14b), and yet He was sitting on the well, being wearied with His journey, when He spoke the life-giving words. Yet again, only Divinity could bid the waves to obey His voice, but a moment or two before He bid them quell their fury His tiredness was acute enough to make the rigging of the boat a soft pillow for His weary head. Surely this is a wonderful blending of the divine and the human.

Round about this ark of dual material was a . . .

Crown of Gold, solid gold. Man had crowned Christ with thorns outside, but now He is inside and there God has eternally crowned Him with glory and honor. The next detail is: "You shall cast . . .

Four Rings of Gold." This enabled the ark to be carried well-balanced. Being of solid gold, these rings apply to the divine side of Christ's character. May we refer to them as four attributes of the divine character, as may also be seen in the four rings of the high priest's breastplate of judgment (Ex. 28:15–30); the two rings on one side of the ark being attributes that are Godward—Justice and Holiness—while the two rings on the other side being attributes that are manward—Grace and Truth. Between the four rings is propitiation. Through these rings passed . . .

Two Poles made of acacia wood and overlaid with gold. Here the two elements are seen again, for Christ as man bore man to God, and as God bore God to man. On the ark was placed the . . .

Mercy Seat. A slab of solid gold two and a half by one and a half cubits. The mercy seat has no wood in it. Propitiation, of which the mercy seat is a type, belongs solely to God. The gold of the mercy seat has been valued at a figure exceeding $25,000. This would make it very precious, but upon it was sprinkled the blood of the atonement which made it priceless.

An extraordinary thing about this mercy seat was

its name, because it was not a seat but a lid. The absence of a seat among the tabernacle furniture is an obvious thing, the reason for this being that there was no need for one. The priestly work was never finished. The priest went on ministering until he was relieved by another, and so in relays the work continued. Only once do we ever read of a priest finishing His work and sitting down. He was the great High Priest. "And every priest *stands* minister-ing daily and offering repeatedly the same sacrifices, which can never take away sins. But this Man, after He had offered one sacrifice for sins forever, *sat down* at the right hand of God" (Heb. 10:11–12). The suggestion implied by the seat is, therefore, that of a finished work. In the administration of the taber-nacle service there was no end. Christ alone could say "It is finished," and when I come to Him I come to the end of my struggling, striving, and all kinds of self-efforts, and rest in Him and on Him. He is the Alpha (the bronze altar) and the Omega (the mercy seat) of our faith.

We note that this was called more than a seat: it was a mercy seat. It was that which covered the law that had been deposited within the ark. Man could not keep it. This was proved when Moses came down from Mount Sinai with the first two tablets of stone and found the people worshiping the golden calf. So then, because man could not keep the law, God cov-ered it with His mercy, and not through our accom-plishments have we found a resting place. We echo the thought of the psalmist when he said: "Surely goodness and mercy shall follow me all the days of my life; and I will dwell in the house of the Lord forever" (Ps. 23:6).

Upon the mercy seat was the blood of propitiation sprinkled there every year on the Day of Atonement. The purpose of the mercy seat was to propitiate, as pointed out in Romans 3:25: "Whom God set forth to be a propitiation [mercy seat] by His blood, through faith, to demonstrate His righteousness, because in His forbearance God had passed over the sins that were previously committed." And yet again in 1 John 4:10: "In this is love, not that we loved God, but that He loved us and sent His Son to be the propitiation [mercy seat] for our sins."

We have yet to consider the . . .

Cherubim. It is cherubim and not cherubims, as quoted in our Authorized Version. Cherubim is the plural of cherub. So we have two cherubim, "one cherub at one end, and the other cherub at the other end; you shall make the cherubim at the two ends of it of one piece with the mercy seat."

These cherubim were one with the mercy seat and of the same material. They are, therefore, inseparable from the propitiatory work of Christ. They have often been looked upon as representative of believers in that we, as believers, are one with Christ, and also in that we are to yield ourselves as willing sacrifices upon the altar. As against this, we point out that the mercy seat is not an altar; there is no sacrifice made upon it. The believer finds himself enjoying fellowship with Christ in front of the ark because he has identified himself with Christ at the altar outside. Again, while it remains true that believers are one with Christ, the position held by these cherubim does not justify the claim here.

Cherubim are symbols of guardianship, as at the gate of the Garden of Eden. Here they are guarding the blood that is sprinkled on the mercy seat. The believer is never called upon to guard the blood; he is ever in need of the blood to guard and to protect him. If the cherubim do not speak in some way of Christ, then the type has broken down on this one point because, not only have we seen Christ in each detail of this sacred chest, but we also shall continue to see Him as we go on to study the contents of the ark.

They symbolize Christ as the Word of God. The "Word" was made flesh and dwelt among men, and the two cherubim remind us of the Living Word and the Written Word, or Christ in all the Scriptures, Old Testament and New Testament. This is wonderfully borne out in the description given: "And they shall face one another." This means agreement, for people turn their backs on those with whom they disagree. We must recognize the fact that the Old and New Testaments agree, the Old foretelling the New and the New fulfilling the Old. The same applies to the written and the living Word. God's Word is in harmony with Christ's life, and Christ came not to destroy the law but to fulfill it.

Though these cherubim face each other, they are not looking at one another—that is, they are not occupied with each other—for "the faces of the cherubim shall be toward the mercy seat." They were looking toward the blood. The Old Testament in type and shadow, in doctrine and example, looks forward to Calvary and the shedding of blood, while the New Testament looks back to Calvary and tells us we are redeemed by the blood of Christ. Their wings are stretched out above, covering the mercy seat. These are the pinions of protection. Men would deny the power of the blood, but the Word of God covers it, keeping it from all its assailants.

Between these cherubim and above the mercy seat was the . . .

Shekinah Glory. The word *Shekinah* does not occur in our Bible at all; it is a Hebrew word. But here, in the Glory Cloud, did the Lord God dwell, and here it was that God met with Israel. It is still the place where God meets man, for that place is between the pages of His Word and on the ground of shed blood.

CHAPTER 17

The Two Tablets of Stone

Exodus 19; 20:1–17. Matthew 22:36–40.

And God spoke all these words, saying: "I am the Lord your God, who brought you out of the land of Egypt, out of the house of bondage. You shall have no other gods before Me.

"You shall not make for yourself any carved image, or any likeness of anything that is in heaven above, or that is in the earth beneath, or that is in the water under the earth; you shall not bow down to them nor serve them. For I, the Lord your God, am a jealous God, visiting the iniquity of the fathers on the children to the third and fourth generations of those who hate Me, but showing mercy to thousands, to those who love Me and keep My commandments.

"You shall not take the name of the Lord your God in vain, for the Lord will not hold him guiltless who takes His name in vain.

"Remember the Sabbath day, to keep it holy. Six days you shall labor and do all your work, but the seventh day is the Sabbath of the Lord your God. In it you shall do no work: you, nor your son, nor your daughter, nor your manservant, nor your maidservant, nor your cattle, nor your stranger who is within your gates. For in six days the Lord made the heavens and the earth, the sea, and all that is in them, and rested the seventh day. Therefore the Lord blessed the Sabbath day and hallowed it.

"Honor your father and your mother, that your days may be long upon the land which the Lord your God is giving you.

"You shall not murder.

"You shall not commit adultery.

"You shall not steal.

"You shall not bear false witness against your neighbor.

"You shall not covet your neighbor's house; you shall not covet your neighbor's wife, nor his manservant, nor his maidservant, nor his ox, nor his donkey, nor anything that is your neighbor's." (Ex. 20:1–17)

"AND you shall put into the ark the Testimony which I will give you." That Testimony was the moral law written on two tablets of stone. The law of God, as given to Moses and as recorded in the Pentateuch, is threefold.

1. The Moral Law. Exodus 20:1–17. This consisted of the Ten Commandments, which we shall be considering in particular. It governed the individual lives of the children of Israel. This section of the law was indelibly engraved on two tablets of stone and was placed under the protection of the mercy seat.

2. The Civil Law. Exodus 21–23. Also Leviticus 11–15 and 17–20. This is what was to control the national life of the children of Israel. It included such laws as those appertaining to murder, property, divorce, servants, injuries, etc. This, with the ceremonial law, was written in a book and kept beside the ark. "So it was, when Moses had completed writing the words of this law in a book, when they were finished, that Moses commanded the Levites, who bore the ark of the covenant of the Lord, saying: 'Take this Book of the Law, and put it beside the ark of the covenant of the Lord your God, that it may be there as a witness against you'" (Deut. 31:24–26).

3. The Ceremonial Law. Exodus 25–31. Also the greater part of Leviticus. This law ordered the religious life of the people. It embraced the subjects of the tabernacle, the priesthood, the offerings, and the feasts.

Looking at the subject still more broadly, one concludes that law was a dispensation; it was the fifth of seven. They are, respectively, the dispensations of: (1) Innocence, (2) Conscience, (3) Human Government, (4) Promise, (5) Law, (6) Grace, (7) The Kingdom.

Let us come back now to the moral law. This was given three times. The first time it was delivered orally. "And God answered him by voice" (Ex. 19:19). "And God spoke all these words, saying . . ." (Ex. 20:1). This statement is followed by the Ten Commandments. In verse 19 the people appealed to Moses, saying, "You speak with us, and we will hear; but let not God speak with us, lest we die." The Apostle Paul referring to the same occasion wrote: ". . . and the sound of a trumpet and the voice of words, so that those who heard it begged that the word should not be spoken to them anymore" (Heb. 12:19).

After this God called Moses to the mount again

that he might receive the law in a written form: "Then the Lord said to Moses, 'Come up to Me on the mountain and be there; and I will give you tablets of stone, and the law and commandments which I have written, that you may teach them'" (Ex. 24:12). It is to be noted that God provided the stones as well as the writing. "Now the tablets were the work of God, and the writing was the writing of God engraved on the tablets" (Ex. 32:16). "He gave Moses two tablets of the Testimony, tablets of stone, written with the finger of God" (Ex. 31:18).

As Moses descended from the mount with Joshua, he heard the noise of singing and beheld that the people below were worshiping a golden calf. Moses looked at the calf and then at the stones in his hands on which he read: "You shall not make for yourself any carved image, or any likeness of anything that is in heaven above, or that is in the earth beneath, or that is in the water under the earth; you shall not bow down to them . . ." (Ex. 20:4–5). He listened and heard the people saying: "This is your god, O Israel, that brought you out of the land of Egypt!" Then looking again at the tablets he saw: "You shall have no other gods before Me." "So Moses' anger became hot, and he cast the tablets out of his hands and broke them at the foot of the mountain" (Ex. 32:19). The law was broken even while it was being made.

We then find that God instructed Moses to procure two more stones. God cut the first pair but He did not make the second. "And the Lord said to Moses, 'Cut two tablets of stone like the first ones, and I will write on these tablets the words that were on the first tablets which you broke. . . .' So he cut two tablets of stone like the first ones. Then Moses rose early in the morning and went up Mount Sinai, as the Lord had commanded him; and he took in his hand the two tablets of stone" (Ex. 34:1, 4). "So he [Moses] was there with the Lord forty days and forty nights; he neither ate bread, nor drank water. And He wrote on the tablets the words of the covenant, the Ten Commandments" (Ex. 34:28).

This law, which man could not keep, was deposited within the ark of the covenant and beneath the mercy seat, the type of the only One who kept the whole law. Moses, reminding the children of Israel of their rebellion, in Deuteronomy 10 says: "At that time the Lord said to me, 'Hew for yourself two tablets of stone like the first, and come up to Me on the mountain and make yourself an ark of wood. And I will write on the tablets the words that were on the first tablets, which you broke; and you shall put them in the ark.' So I made an ark of acacia wood, hewed two tablets of stone like the first, and went up the mountain, having the two tablets in my hand. And He wrote on the tablets according to the first writing, the Ten Commandments, which the Lord had spoken to you in the mountain from the midst of the fire in the day of the assembly; and the Lord gave them to me. Then I turned and came down from the mountain, and put the tablets in the ark which I had made; and there they are, just as the Lord commanded me" (vv. 1–5).

A further point of interest in these tablets is that

they were written upon back and front. "And Moses turned and went down from the mountain, and the two tablets of the Testimony were in his hand. The tablets were written on both sides; on the one side and on the other they were written" (Ex. 32:15). Should not this often overlooked statement remind us that the law cannot be evaded? Man is full of excuses and might suggest to God that he did not know the law—that he had seen only the back side of the tablets. But not so. Wherever man is, he must face up to the law; if not, the law will face up with him. "Therefore you are inexcusable, O man, whoever you are . . ." (Rom. 2:1). I cannot evade the law, but I can escape it—but only by being hidden in *Christ* who is willing to fulfill it on my behalf.

What was the object of writing the Decalogue on two tablets of stone and not one? It was not for reason of size, because the stones were small enough for Moses to carry them up the mount and down the mount together. Was it not because the commandments were divided into two distinct sections? The possibility is there were four commandments on one stone and the remaining six on the other stone. It is but a preconceived idea to put five on each stone. We are not told how they were divided, but we have good reason to believe they were four and six. The first four commandments reveal man's duty to God:

1. His Person: No other gods before Me.
2. His Worship: No graven image or likeness to be made or worshiped.
3. His Name: Not to be used wrongfully.
4. His Day: It must be kept holy.

The last six commandments show us man's duty to man:

    5. Shall honor parents.
    6. Shall not kill another.
    7. Shall not commit adultery with another.
    8. Shall not steal from another.
    9. Shall not tell lies against another.
    10. Shall not covet the possessions of another.

The whole of the law appears to be thus condensed and thus divided by Christ Himself in answer to the lawyer who asked for the greatest commandment. "Jesus said to him, '"You shall love the Lord your God with all your heart, with all your soul, and with all your mind." This is the first and great commandment [first stone]. And the second is like it: "You shall love your neighbor as yourself [second stone]." On these two commandments hang *all* the Law and the Prophets'" (Matt. 22:37–40).

The subject of the law is very vast, so we will endeavor to summarize it in a few quotations from the Scriptures:

1. It Reveals Sin (Rom. 3:20): "Therefore by the deeds of the law no flesh will be justified in His sight, for by the law is the knowledge of sin."

2. It Cannot Justify (Gal. 2:16): "Knowing that a man is not justified by the works of the law but by faith in Jesus Christ, even we have believed in Christ Jesus, that we might be justified by faith in Christ and not by the works of the law; for by the works of the law no flesh shall be justified."

3. It Leads to Christ (Gal. 3:24–25): "Therefore

the law was our tutor to bring us to Christ, that we might be justified by faith. But after faith has come, we are no longer under a tutor." This we can see working in every phase of life. The driving instructor is a tutor who brings me to the knowledge of driving. When the knowledge has come, I no longer need a tutor but I go on driving with my newly acquired knowledge.

4. It Is Eternal (Luke 16:17): "And it is easier for heaven and earth to pass away than for one tittle of the law to fail."

5. It Was Made Weak Through the Flesh (Rom. 8:3): "For what the law could not do in that it was weak through the flesh, God did by sending His own Son in the likeness of sinful flesh, on account of sin: He condemned sin in the flesh." It must not be understood here that the flesh first referred to is to the Adamic nature or the human nature. That did not weaken a perfect and eternal law. It was the flesh of the animals offered as substitutes for sin under the law that was weak. The offerings could atone for sin—temporarily cover sin—but they could not justify or redeem the sinner because an animal does not know temptation and does not possess sinful flesh. The law, therefore, came short of man's need, so God sent His Son in the likeness of *sinful flesh* to condemn sin in the flesh.

6. It Was Fulfilled in Christ (Matt. 5:17): "Do not think that I came to destroy the Law or the Prophets. I did not come to destroy but to fulfill." If we have an engagement and fail to keep it, we have broken our promise; but if we fulfill that engagement, the promise then ceases to exist. This is exactly what has happened with the law. Christ did not break any of its precepts, but He did fulfill its demands. It demanded death—He met that demand and died. The law is, therefore, fulfilled, and there is no death now to the person who believes it, for . . .

7. Christ Is the End of the Law, to believers only (Rom. 10:4): "For Christ is the end of the law for righteousness to every one who believes." That means, therefore, that . . .

8. We Are Not Under the Law (Rom. 6:14): "For sin shall not have dominion over you, for you are not under law but under grace." This does not mean that the law does not exist. It means that I am insulated. An electric cable would injure and perhaps kill one who touched it, but if that person were to stand on a rubber mat and wear heavy rubber gloves he would be insulated; and while the power would remain, it would not harm him. So is it with the law and the man who has put on Christ Jesus as Lord. "Therefore if the Son makes you free, you shall be free indeed" (John 8:36). We must not use our liberty as a cloak for maliciousness, for . . .

9. We Are a Law to Ourselves (Rom. 2:14): "For when Gentiles, who do not have the law, by nature do the things contained in the law, these, although not having the law, are a law to themselves." In Christ there is neither Jew nor Gentile, but to the Christian there is a law of love and obedience. The old law said "Do and live"—the law of grace says "Live, and do."

· CHAPTER 18 ·

The Golden Pot of Manna

Exodus 16:11–36. Numbers 11:1–9. Psalm 78:24–25.
John 6:31–58. Revelation 2:17.

And the Lord spoke to Moses, saying, "I have heard
the murmurings of the children of Israel. Speak to them,
saying, 'At twilight you shall eat meat, and in the morning you shall be filled with bread. And you shall know
that I am the Lord your God.'"

So it was that quails came up at evening and covered
the camp, and in the morning the dew lay all around the
camp. And when the layer of dew lifted, there, on the
surface of the wilderness, was a small round substance, as
fine as frost on the ground. So when the children of Israel saw it, they said to one another, "What is it?" For
they did not know what it was. And Moses said to them,
"This is the bread which the Lord has given you to eat.
This is the thing which the Lord has commanded: 'Let
every man gather it according to each one's need, one
omer for each person, according to the number of persons; let every man take for those who are in his tent.'"
And the children of Israel did so and gathered, some
more, some less. So when they measured it by omers, he
who gathered much had nothing over, and he who gathered little had no lack. Every man had gathered according to each one's need. And Moses said, "Let no one

leave any of it till morning." Notwithstanding they did not heed Moses. But some of them left part of it until morning, and it bred worms and stank. And Moses was angry with them. So they gathered it every morning, every man according to his need. And when the sun became hot, it melted.

And so it was, on the sixth day, that they gathered twice as much bread, two omers for each one. And all the rulers of the congregation came and told Moses. Then he said to them, "This is what the Lord has said: 'Tomorrow is a Sabbath rest, a holy Sabbath to the Lord. Bake what you will bake today, and boil what you will boil; and lay up for yourselves all that remains, to be kept until morning.'" So they laid it up till morning, as Moses commanded; and it did not stink, nor were there any worms in it. Then Moses said, "Eat that today, for today is a Sabbath to the Lord; today you will not find it in the field. Six days you shall gather it, but on the seventh day, which is the Sabbath, there will be none." Now it happened that some of the people went out on the seventh day to gather, but they found none. And the Lord said to Moses, "How long do you refuse to keep My commandments and My laws? See! For the Lord has given you the Sabbath; therefore He gives you on the sixth day bread for two days. Let every man remain in his place; let no man go out of his place on the seventh day." So the people rested on the seventh day. And the house of Israel called its name Manna. And it was like white coriander seed, and the taste of it was like wafers made with honey. (Ex. 16:11–31)

Now the manna was like coriander seed, and its color like the color of bdellium. The people went about and gathered it, ground it on millstones or beat it in the mortar, cooked it in pans, and made cakes of it; and its taste was like the taste of pastry prepared with oil. And when the dew fell on the camp in the night, the manna fell on it. (Num. 11:7–9)

WHEN the children of Israel first saw the bread of God's providing they said: "It is manna." There are three interpretations to the word "manna." They are:

Hebrew............................ "What is it?"
Chaldean ...."It is a portion."
English .... "Bread."

The people were soon to learn what it really was. It was to be their food while they journeyed. Jesus said that He was the "Bread of Life." He also said: "I am the true bread . . . the living bread which came down from heaven." The world still looks on, and of Christ and the Word of God they are saying: "What is it?" The true believer is he who can use the word in the Chaldean sense and say concerning the Word of God: "It is a portion," and concerning Christ Himself: "He is a portion."

What kind of a portion was the manna to this army of pilgrims? It was a . . .

Sufficient Portion. There was enough for all and no lack.

Suitable Portion. It suited every palate, young and old alike, also the weak and the strong. The Jews say, "It tasted to every man as he pleased."

Satisfying Portion. No man ever went hungry. "The young lions lack and suffer hunger; but those who seek the Lord shall not lack any good thing."

Strengthening Portion. It made strong men of them.

They were able to journey in a desert, to work, and to fight.

Sustaining Portion. On it they lived for forty years. It must have been very nutritious.

Sure Portion. It never failed.

Cannot all this be said of Christ Jesus our Lord? There is an all-sufficiency in Him. He suits all classes, all nationalities, all ages, yea, all men everywhere. He certainly satisfies those who trust Him. "All that I want is in Jesus; He satisfies, joy He supplies. Life would be worthless without Him. All things in Jesus I find." He also strengthens His followers for life and service. He will sustain us all through life's journey and will never fail. Joshua tells us that there was an overlap in the supply of manna. "Now the manna ceased on the day after they had eaten the produce of the land" (Josh. 5:12). Christ is not only our supply in life but He will take us through until we get right into the heavenly land to feast upon "hidden manna."

What a wonderful description is given to us of so small an object. This is because it is typical of Christ as the Bread of Life, and the description shows forth His character, as follows:

Description	Type
Small	Humility of Christ.
Round	Perfection of His Life.
White	Purity of His character.
Like Frost	Crisp, energizing the life He imparts.

Like Coriander Seed: . . .

    (a) Aromatic when crushed .... Fragrance of the
                                        suffering Man of Calvary.

    (b) A herb ...... Health of mankind.

As fresh oil .... Anointing of the Holy Spirit.

As honey .... Sweetness of the "Word of God."

As bdellium .... "The Pearl of Greatest Price."

This is a matchless picture of the Christ whom we serve. Has not God promised to supply all our needs according to His riches in glory by Christ Jesus! Well may we sing:

> "I've found the Pearl of Greatest Price,
> My heart doth sing for joy;
> And sing I must, for Christ I have—
> Oh! what a Christ have I!
> Christ is my Meat, Christ is my Drink,
> My Medicine and my Health,
> My Portion, mine Inheritance,
> Yea, all my Boundless Wealth."

We will now consider . . .

How It Came. (1) *Every morning.* In the manna we see Christ as both the "Living Word" and the "Written Word," but more particularly as the latter. As "a portion" we see Him in both ways. In the description of the manna He is seen as the "Living Word." But now in the instructions we see Him as the "Written Word." The Lord would encourage us in a daily reading of His Word, and that at the beginning of the day.

(2) *Around the camp.* That is, it was within the

reach of all. There is a community of people that put the Church on earth in a place superior to the Bible. They would tell us that their *Church* has received full and final authority—that the Bible alone is inadequate. This would mean that some could never get a daily supply from God: sickness, business, distance, weather, and a score of other reasons might prevent a person from obtaining daily spiritual sustenance. But God has given us His Word in the form of a written oracle or a book. It is in the camp; it is always within reach.

(3) *With the dew.* "And when the dew fell on the camp in the night, the manna fell on it" (Num. 11:9). "And when the layer of dew lifted, there, on the surface of the wilderness, was a small round substance, as fine as the frost on the ground" (Ex. 16:14). It would appear from these two scriptures that the dew was both underneath and on the top of the manna, thus enwrapping it and keeping it fresh and clean. It was the moving of the dew that revealed the manna. The dew is one of the symbols of the Holy Spirit. I may have the Word of God within my reach. I may read it and *not* profit thereby. Carnal and critical minds never do benefit from thus reading. It was when the dew lifted that the manna was revealed, and it is by the moving of the Spirit that divine revelation comes to us. For "when He, the Spirit of truth, has come, *He* will guide you into all truth . . ." (John 16:13).

God then gave a number of . . .

Instructions to control the allocation of the divine provision.

(1) *The head of the house was to gather for all within.* "This is the thing which the Lord has commanded: 'Let every man gather it according to each one's need, an omer for each person, according to the number of persons; let every man take for those who are in his tent'" (Ex. 16:16). "According to each one's need" means according to the size of his family. It is important to note that the Lord told the *men* to gather for those inside his tent, namely, the women and the children. In the Middle East the women do much of the manual and the menial work, grinding grain, drawing water, etc., but here the man is instructed so to do. Not only is it the duty and the privilege of the man, as the head of the house, to collect and distribute spiritual food at the morning reading and prayers of the family, but it is the duty of us all to minister to those who cannot gather for themselves. In this injunction comes a great call for family worship.

(2) *At the rate of an omer per head.* It was an equal portion for all. It was as much for the maid as for the mistress, and for the servant as the master; as much for the women as for the men. It was equally as much for the child and for "your stranger who is within your gates."

(3) *One day's portion at a time (except the sixth day).* God's gifts are always given as needed. The harvest of the whole world has an overlap of only six weeks. We live by faith. God has promised to meet our needs day by day, and He will not fail us. Because no manner of work was to be done on the Sabbath day, He made provision on the sixth day for a double

supply. God always will provide for the man who honors Him by the keeping of the Lord's day, the one in seven. We are now living in an age when the Lord's day is being sadly neglected by the world and slackly used by the Church. Christians now do business on Sunday without any concern. They stay away from the house of God to cook the dinner. They write and mail letters on a Sunday, which could easily be done on Monday, but as a result they are losing much of the joy of the Lord. God must and will honor those who honor Him.

Looking at the matter more broadly, one may meet a period in life when the source of outward supply is cut off temporarily by uncontrollable circumstances. Then we shall find that God has given us a source of inward supply that has unconsciously come to us through the faithful gathering of the past.

(4) *None were to have a surplus*. God never encouraged a storing up, for that indicated either selfishness or lack of trust. Some people seem to find surplus. They will refer to certain parts of God's Word, or to some doctrines, principles or commands, as unnecessary—something with which they can do without. The modernist appears to find a good deal of surplus in the Bible. God says there is nothing over—that every word is profitable, and is for our learning. But while there is no surplus, God is not stingy, for . . .

(5) *None were to lack anything* (v. 18). God gives according to our ability. Believing that I shall lack nothing, I must use all. The writer remembers an occasion when, as a lad just beginning to speak in

open-air meetings and in small ways, he received one day a blessing and a message from the Word of God. He was so pleased about it that he decided not to pass it on but to keep it for some special occasion when he might be asked to speak at a larger meeting; but when the "larger meeting" came he could not remember that message. He tried hard, but he had forgotten it. He had lost it. It had "bred worms and stank." He learned his lesson as a lad, and since then has always sought at all times to give the best.

(6) *The sun cleansed the earth after the morning gathering*. This surely tells us to make much of present opportunities or we may lose everything.

Methods of Use. "Bake what you will bake today, and boil what you will boil . . ." (Ex. 16:23b). "The people went about and gathered it, and ground it on millstones or beat it in the mortar, cooked it in pans, and made cakes of it . . ." (Num. 11:8). From these two verses we see that a variety of methods were used in preparing the manna for consumption. It could be ground in the handmills like wheat, or it could be crushed in the mortar. It could be baked or cooked in a pot, or made into cakes for the child. We may classify it in this way:

Baked .... for the strong ...... Strong meat.
Seethed .... for the weaker ..... Bread.
Ground or Beaten . for the simple
                                     or aged......... Sincere milk.
Made into cakes .. for the child .... Royal dainties.

We may take the Word of God and study it as we will for profit: dispensationally or doctrinally for the strong in faith; book, text or character for the weaker in faith; or the parables, stories and miracles of Christ for the young in faith. We may take the Bible and grind it up, breaking it as small as we wish, as the botanist does with his analysis of the flower and the chemist with his chemistry. We shall profit by so doing, *but* we must not tear the Book up and pull it to pieces as the critic and the modernist do. Honest criticism is good and profitable; critical criticism is wrong and disastrous. This is seen in rather an extraordinary way in our lesson, for the manna would stand beating and grinding; yet, after the rising of the morning sun, it disappeared like the dew. Divine revelation and knowledge will always flee before the rays of modernistic and materialistic thought, leaving the thinkers starving and dissatisfied, not because it is afraid or cannot face the modernist but because ". . . You have hidden these things from the wise and prudent and have revealed them to babes" (Matt. 11:25).

Final Application. Christ very ably showed Himself to be the great antitype of the manna in John 6. The Jews had always given Moses the credit for supplying their forefathers with the manna in the wilderness. Alas, God is still often robbed of glory and praise of which He alone is worthy. So Jesus reasons with the crowd, and says, "Most assuredly, I say to you, Moses did not give you the bread from heaven, but My Father gives you the true bread from heaven. For the bread of God is He who comes down from heaven and gives life to the world. . . . I am the bread of life. He who comes to Me shall never hunger, and he who believes on Me shall never thirst. . . . I am the bread of life. Your fathers ate the manna in the wilderness, and are dead. This is the bread which comes down from heaven, that one may eat of it and not die. I am the living bread which came down from heaven. If anyone eats of this bread, he will live forever; and the bread that I shall give is My flesh, which I shall give for the life of the world. . . . Most assuredly, I say to you, unless you eat the flesh of the Son of Man and drink His blood, you have no life in you. Whoever eats My flesh and drinks My blood has eternal life, and I will raise him up at the last day. For My flesh is food indeed, and My blood is drink indeed" (John 6:32–55).

A final scripture is in Revelation 2:17: ". . .To him who overcomes I will give some of the hidden manna to eat. . . ." While we enjoy many revealed blessings of Christ and His Word, there remain many things which we do not yet understand. Though we do not understand them, we must not deny them or disbelieve them. If we remain faithful to the things we have and overcome through His blood and Word, the promise is that by and by we shall feast upon these hidden glories which will then be revealed.

" 'Take a pot and put an omer of manna in it, and lay it up before the Lord, to be kept for your generations.' As the Lord commanded Moses, so Aaron laid it up before the Testimony, to be kept" (Ex. 16:33–34).

So it became part of the contents of the ark of God.

CHAPTER 19

Aaron's Rod that Budded

Numbers 16 and 17.

And the Lord spoke to Moses, saying: "Speak to the children of Israel, and get from them a rod from each father's house, all their leaders according to their fathers' houses—twelve rods. Write each man's name on his rod. And you shall write Aaron's name on the rod of Levi. For there shall be one rod for the head of each father's house. Then you shall place them in the tabernacle of meeting before the Testimony, where I meet with you. And it shall be that the rod of the man whom I choose will blossom; thus I will rid Myself of the murmurings of the children of Israel, which they murmur against you."

So Moses spoke to the children of Israel, and each of their leaders gave him a rod apiece, for each leader according to their fathers' houses, twelve rods; and the rod of Aaron was among their rods. And Moses placed the rods before the Lord in the tabernacle of witness.

Now it came to pass on the next day that Moses went into the tabernacle of witness, and behold, the rod of Aaron, of the house of Levi, had sprouted and put forth buds, had produced blossoms and yielded ripe almonds. Then Moses brought out all the rods from before the Lord to all the children of Israel; and they looked, and each man took his rod.

And the Lord said to Moses, "Bring Aaron's rod back before the Testimony, to be kept as a sign against the rebels, that you may put their murmurings away from Me, lest they die." Thus did Moses; just as the Lord had commanded him, so he did.

And the children of Israel spoke to Moses, saying, "Surely we die, we perish, we all perish! Whoever even comes near the tabernacle of the Lord must die. Shall we all utterly die?" (Num. 17)

THE third and final token found within the ark was the rod of Aaron that budded, blossomed, and brought forth almonds. This was the emblem of a God-chosen priesthood.

The Context. The story, which occupies two chapters of the book of Numbers, tells of Korah, Dathan, and Abiram, who gathered together two hundred and fifty of the leading men of Israel in rebellion against Moses and Aaron. The accusation, which was a false one, was that Moses had overstepped the mark: he had usurped his authority; he was full of pride; and in calling in Aaron his brother as priest he had made Israel's leadership a family concern. The accusation stands in marked contrast to God's thought concerning Moses, which was: "Now the man Moses was very humble, more than all men who were on the face of the earth" (Num. 12:3). Moses did the wisest thing it is possible to do when misjudged and misrepresented. He took it straight to the Lord.

God commanded that all the two hundred and fifty-three men should present themselves before Him the next day, and as they had asserted that they too could be priests they were to bring, each man, a priestly instrument, namely, a censer containing live fire and incense. After an exchange of accusations and reproof, God spoke. He declared that He would destroy the whole host, but Moses pleaded with God that they should not all die for one man's sin.

God then told the people to separate themselves from the tents of the three leaders of the revolt, while Moses stood and addressed the assembly, saying, "By this you shall know that the Lord has sent me to do all these works, for I have not done them of my own will. If these men die naturally like all men, or if they are visited by the common fate of all men, then the Lord has not sent me. But if the Lord creates a new thing, and the earth opens its mouth and swallows them up with all that belongs to them, and they go down alive into the pit, then you will understand that these men have rejected the Lord" (Num. 16:28–30). Moses had barely finished this speech when the ground split apart and these men and their families were swallowed alive. What a picture of the proverb, "He who is often reproved, and hardens his neck, will suddenly be destroyed, and that without remedy" (Prov. 29:1). And what a fulfillment of "Heaven and earth shall pass away, but My words shall not pass away." These men were opposing the Word of God through Moses, but found the earth slipping from beneath their feet.

At the very time God was punishing the three men, a fire broke out and consumed the two hun-

dred and fifty leaders who had rebelled with them.
From the burning embers the censers had to be res-
cued because they had been hallowed.

Instead of repenting, the whole assembly blamed
Moses for the slaughter, so that God's indignation
was further increased—and the next day a plague
broke out which would have destroyed all if Moses
and Aaron had not stood between the living and
the dead and made an atonement. The cost of that
rebellion against the servants of the Lord was approximately fifteen thousand lives.

God then proceeded to give the people a further
evidence of the fact that He had chosen Aaron as
the High Priest, and so vindicated the characters of
His servants.

The leaders of the twelve tribes were each to bring
a rod upon which Moses was to write the man's name.
Moses was to present their rods before God by bringing them into the tabernacle and leaving them there
overnight. The Lord said that the rod of the man He
would choose would blossom. Next morning Moses
went in to see the rods, and there he found one out
of the twelve with buds, blossoms, and ripe almonds
upon it. The name on that rod was Aaron, for the
tribe of Levi. Every man was given back his rod; his
name being on the rod prevented any discrepancy.
The Lord then said, "Bring Aaron's rod back before
the Testimony, to be kept as a sign against the rebels."
The Apostle Paul, writing to the Hebrews, said that
the rod was inside the ark, as also the pot of manna
and the two tablets of the covenant.

So much for the story concerning Aaron's rod,

but now as to its meaning. It is clear from the foregoing that it represents a God-chosen priesthood. The evidences of such a priesthood are threefold. (1) Buds, the symbol of life. (2) Blossoms, the token of beauty. (3) Fruit, the sign of usefulness. There are three different priesthoods in Scripture which we will test by this God-given sign as to whether they are God-chosen.

1. Aaron Chosen by God for Israel. The sign of the budding rod appears to have satisfied Israel. We never hear of them questioning his right again after this. Perhaps the sign was a fit symbol of the life of Aaron.

Buds. Life came to a dead stick. The twelve rods laid up before the Lord were barren and had no contact with the earth, so the life that entered this one stick, causing it to bud, must have come from above. We feel sure that Aaron must have known something of a new life, a heaven-born life, or he would not have been chosen for such a position.

Blossoms. God is the author of beauty. God looks for beauty of character, which is a gem far above rubies and diamonds in value. There was undoubtedly fragrance of character here, for God to choose this man.

Almonds. These betoken fruitfulness and wakefulness. Aaron must have been a man alert to responsibility and duty, a man upon whom God could depend.

In the natural, the bud gives place to the flower and the flower dies to make room for the fruit. But in this rod Moses found it productive of all three at once. So it is in the spiritual realm. The Christian is never asked to forfeit the bud of new life, new joy, new love, new emotions. We are sometimes told to get back to our first love. Neither does a Christian have to discard beauty of character for usefulness in service.

2. Christ Chosen by God for the Church. Christ claimed to be a priest of the Melchizedek order. Was He chosen by God, or did He take it upon Himself? If the sign of the rod satisfied Israel it ought to satisfy us, so we will examine His life accordingly.

A Rod. This is what God used. This is what Christ was. The prophet said He was a root out of dry ground; had no form, no comeliness, no beauty to be desired. This "rod," like Aaron's, was presented with others before God. There were twelve all told with Aaron's rod, but only three when Christ was presented. He Himself and two criminals stood, or hung, before God, men, and demons. They all three died.

Buds. The third day life descended from above and entered into one of those three sticks, the one that bore the name of "priest," and He burst the bands of death and came forth into the newness of resurrection life. Up from the grave He arose!

Blossoms. The fragrance of that resurrection life is seen in His post-resurrection movements as He appeared here and there, leaving wonderful words of cheer and hope to the crestfallen disciples whose hopes had been shattered by the death of their Lord a few days previously.

Almonds. The fruit of that resurrection life can be found in the words of the Lord as He says, "I am the firstfruits of those who sleep; as I live you shall live also."

3. Believers Chosen by God for the Unsaved. We, as believers, are priests and belong to a royal priesthood. Let us look for the symbol, and so see whether we are God-chosen.

A Rod. The Bible declares that there is none good, that we are dead in trespasses and sins. In this condition we were brought into touch with Christ. We heard the way of salvation, we believed, and the result was:

Buds. Life came from above, entered into our dead souls, and we began to live. The life we now live we live by faith in the Son of God. It is Christ dwelling in us. Therefore, there ought to be:

Blossoms. Beauty of character, beauty of walk, beauty of holiness. Ours should be a life which, by its fragrance, should draw others to Christ. Our prayer and aim should be:

> "Let the beauty of Jesus be seen in me,
> All His wondrous compassion and purity.
> Oh! Thou Spirit Divine, all my nature refine,
> Till the beauty of Jesus be seen in me."

This will mean:

Almonds, or the life of fruitfulness. We ought to be bearing the fruit of the Spirit which is Love, Joy, Peace, Longsuffering, Kindness, Goodness, Faithfulness, Gentleness and Self-control. This fruit should be ever increasing. According to John 15 it is fruit, more fruit, much fruit, and fruit that remains.

If we, as priests, intercede with God, the fruit will be souls eternally saved, hearts continuously blessed, Christians constantly uplifted.

Chosen in Him.

· CHAPTER 20 ·

The Journeyings of the Ark

1. From Sinai to Philistia

Exodus 25 and 40. Numbers 3, 4, 10 and 14. Joshua 3,
4, 6 and 7. 1 Samuel 3 and 4. Psalm 132.

Lord, remember David and all his afflictions; how he
swore to the Lord, and vowed to the Mighty God of Jacob:
"Surely I will not go into the chamber of my house, or go
up to the comfort of my bed; I will not give sleep to my
eyes or slumber to my eyelids, until I find a place for the
Lord, a dwelling place for the Mighty God of Jacob."

Behold, we heard of it in Ephrathah; we found it in
the fields of the woods. Let us go into His tabernacle; let
us worship at His footstool. Arise, O Lord, to Your resting place, You and the ark of Your strength. Let Your
priests be clothed with righteousness, and let Your saints
shout for joy.

For Your servant David's sake, do not turn away the
face of Your Anointed.

The Lord has sworn in truth to David; He will not
turn from it: "I will set upon your throne the fruit of your
body. If your sons will keep My covenant and My testimony which I shall teach them, their sons also shall sit
upon your throne forevermore."

For the Lord has chosen Zion; He has desired it for His

habitation: "This is My resting place forever; here I will dwell, for I have desired it. I will abundantly bless her provision; I will satisfy her poor with bread. I will also clothe her priests with salvation, and her saints shall shout aloud for joy. There I will make the horn of David grow; I will prepare a lamp for My Anointed. His enemies I will clothe with shame, but upon Himself His crown shall flourish." (Ps. 132)

WE often hear the remark that the Old Testament is dry and uninteresting. That really depends upon the reader and how he approaches the Book. The story of the journeyings of the ark can be as thrilling and as exciting as any adventure story written in fiction. "Truth *is* stranger than fiction!"

The ark of the covenant carried with it the power of the God it represented. This power was from time to time manifested as it moved from place to place. But before we travel with it, it will be necessary to make one or two observations.

The psalm which precedes this chapter is one of the Songs of Ascents and was sung by the people as they journeyed with the ark before them. The ark was . . .

Built at Sinai by Bezaleel and his workmen, who were skilled in all manner of workmanship because they were controlled by the Spirit of God. There is a thought just here. It is not the preacher and the minister only who need the Spirit of God resting upon them. God has promised His Spirit to all believers, so that, it matters not what the nature of our service is, we may know the help and guidance of the Holy Spirit. The ark did not become a sacred shrine until it was placed in the . . .

Holy of Holies. Then it was that the glory of the *Shekinah* presence of the Lord rested upon it. "And he brought the ark into the tabernacle, hung up the veil of the covering, and partitioned off the ark of the Testimony. . . . So Moses finished the work. Then the cloud covered the tabernacle of meeting, and the glory of the Lord filled the tabernacle" (Ex. 40:21, 33–34).

In all its journeyings the ark was . . .

Carried by the Kohathites (Num. 3:30–31). They were one of the clans of the tribe of Levi, whose special burden was the ark, the lampstand, the table of showbread, and the two altars, with all their vessels—and possibly the laver, but this is never mentioned.

Its Appearance (Num. 4:5–6): "When the camp prepares to journey, Aaron and his sons shall come, and they shall take down the covering veil and cover the ark of the Testimony with it. Then they shall put on it a covering of badger skins, and spread over that a cloth entirely of blue; and they shall insert its poles." All that the people saw, therefore, was a blue burden being borne upon the shoulders. This stood in contrast to all the other furniture, which was covered first by either a blue, purple, or scarlet cloth and, afterwards, badgers' skins.

We now follow their travels.

The First Move (Num. 10:33): "So they departed from the mountain of the Lord on a journey of three days; and the ark of the covenant of the Lord went before them for the three days' journey, to search out a resting place for them." Except for the next reference we shall consider, no more is said concerning the ark in all their forty years of traveling and wandering in the wilderness. This verse stands as an example. To put it again and again would only be unnecessary repetition. In this instance they journeyed three days. Sometimes they did more and sometimes they did less, but the ark always went before them. Whenever the ark set out, Moses said, "Rise up, O Lord! Let Your enemies be scattered, and let those who hate You flee before You." And when it rested, he said, "Return, O Lord, to the many thousands of Israel" (Num. 10:35–36).

This is the same ark that we have seen typifying Christ in all its construction. When we journey, the Lord will go before us. He will keep us in all our ways, He will lead us by a right path; and when we rest, it is He who makes us to lie down in green pastures. We are able to say: "God is in the midst of us; we shall not be moved."

This first example is to show us the joy of having God leading the way. The next and only other example in the wilderness is the reverse. What happens if He does not lead the way?

Absence Means Defeat (Num. 14). The camp had arrived at Kadesh Barnea. They had been safely brought across the wilderness. From here spies were sent ahead to spy out the land of Canaan, with the result that ten returned with a bad report despite the evidence, and two returned with a good report and tangible evidence that they were speaking the truth, for they brought with them a great cluster of grapes which they bore on a pole, and also some pomegranates and figs. The people, with hearts full of doubt, ignored this practical demonstration and believed the words of the ten spies. They wept all night, and chided Moses and Aaron for bringing them to a place of death.

The Lord's wrath was kindled against the people because this was the tenth time they had provoked Him, and He said He would disinherit them. But once again Moses wonderfully prevailed with God in prayer and intercession. So instead of destroying them, He turned them southward, with their backs toward the promised land, into the wilderness again, by way of the Red Sea—there to wander for forty years until all had died except Joshua and Caleb, the two worthy spies who, with a later generation, would enter the land.

When God said "Go up," they refused; so God declared: "Just as you have spoken, you shall not go up; but you shall perish in the wilderness." Then they mourned and said, "We will go up." "They rose early in the morning and went up to the top of the mountain, saying, 'Here we are, and we will go up to the place which the Lord has promised, for we have sinned!' Then Moses said, 'Now why do you transgress the command of the Lord? For this will not succeed. Do not go up, lest you be defeated by your enemies. . . .' But they presumed to go up to the mountaintop; nevertheless, neither the ark of the covenant of the Lord nor Moses departed from the camp. Then the Amalekites and the Canaanites who dwelt in that mountain came down and attacked them, and drove them back as far as Hormah" (Num. 14:40–45).

What lessons for us to learn! First, rebellion and disobedience are disastrous and, second, if God is not with us, how helpless we are. We must always follow Christ and never go ahead of Him or we will meet trouble.

After forty years expired, once more the children of Israel stood at the borders of the desired land. Between them and their promised possession was the swift current of the Jordan River. But the ark . . .

Parts Jordan (Josh. 3 and 4). Years before, after one stroke from the rod of Moses, God parted asunder the Red Sea—a type of salvation. But here at Jordan things were different. This time it was a step-by-step walk of faith.

The long-anticipated day had come. What a day of excitement! What a day of commands and instructions! What a day of obedience! They were not going to have a repetition of the evil day forty years previously. The officers commanded the people, saying: "When you see the ark of the covenant of the Lord your God, and the priests, the Levites, bearing it, then you shall set out from your place and go after it" (Josh. 3:3). Then Joshua spoke to the priests, saying, "Take up the ark of the covenant and cross over before the people." So they took up the ark of the covenant and went before the people. Then the priests came and stood with the ark on their shoulders, and put their feet in the water of the overflowing banks, while Joshua cried, "Behold, the ark of the covenant of the Lord of all the earth is crossing over before you into the Jordan" (Josh. 3:11). The priests proceeded into the waters of the Jordan, and as they did the floodwaters ceased. "Then the priests who bore the ark of the covenant of the Lord stood firm on dry ground in the midst of the Jordan; and all Israel crossed over on dry ground, until all the people had crossed completely over the Jordan" (Josh. 3:17).

Twelve chosen men followed, and each took a stone from the bed of the river where the priests had stood with the ark, and with the stones on their shoulders they went over to the other side. The priests came up following the twelve men, and as their feet touched the bank of the river the waters returned to their place. The twelve stones were erected at Gilgal between the Jordan and Jericho, where the people camped that night. They were now in the land.

Here we learn that whatever the obstacle, or however impossible the command of the Lord to us may appear, if it is His command He will see us safely through. Barriers must fall and problems melt before the presence of the "Ark" of our salvation.

While at Gilgal the Passover was observed, and the manna, hitherto so regularly given, now ceased. Then came the next move forward. The ark . . .

Takes Jericho (Josh. 6). Two spies had been into the city, and rumor was current in Jericho that the Israelites were approaching. Travelers to the city had possibly brought news of the doings of these people and how they had crossed the Jordan. The city was, therefore, securely shut up. Its walls were very formidable—although not as formidable as the ten spies had once said, for they did not reach up to heaven, and the citizens were not quite giants! Nevertheless, they had the advantage of the walls, a high position, and gates, whereas the Israelites had nothing—except God, and what an exception! He was a great Captain. The leader—Joshua—now issued the commands of the Captain. The ark of the covenant was to be carried around the city walls, preceded by seven priests with seven trumpets and followed by all of Israel's men of war. This was to be done once each day for six days, and on the seventh day they were to march around seven times. Throughout these marches the men were not allowed to speak a word. It was not to be what they *thought* but what God had *said* that would bring them the victory. Then, with a blast of trumpets and a shout of triumph, down went the walls, out went the enemy, in went Israel. We must notice that the men shouted before the walls fell. It was a shout of faith.

We learn that God never removes the things that test our faith; Jericho had to be met even after forty years. The Lord will give us faith to stand the test if we let Him.

Unfortunately, sin came into the camp through the disobedience of Achan. We now see that the ark . . .

Humbles the Believer (Josh. 7:6): "Then Joshua tore his clothes, and fell to the earth on his face before the ark of the Lord until the evening, both he and the elders of Israel; and they put dust on their heads." God had done the previous work and had given them a magnificent victory, but the men of Israel had taken to themselves the glory of it by soon afterward estimating their own physical ability, quite leaving God out of the reckoning. "Do not let all the people go up," they had said, "but let about two or three thousand men go up and attack Ai. Do not weary all the people there, for the people of Ai are few" (Josh. 7:13). But instead of capturing the town they were defeated and lost thirty-six men. A Babylonian garment, two hundred shekels of silver and a wedge of gold were the price for which their victory was sold. So Joshua stretched himself before the Lord in humility until God made known the reason.

It was secret sin, and that only in one man. And more, the one man was not the leader but one of the rank and file. Has it ever occurred to you that a fault in one ordinary member of the church can rob the whole assembly of blessing and bring spiritual defeat? So often when a church is not prospering, or any Christian work is failing to make advancement, we look at the minister or the leader for the cause. Maybe we ought to look at ourselves.

We now pass on to the time of Eli, the priest, and find the ark of God . . .

At Shiloh (1 Sam. 1:3; 3:3). This was the permanent pitch of the tabernacle until the time when Solomon built the temple and the "curtains" were required no more. We are here introduced to the tabernacle set up within the land at a very dark time in Israel's history. Eli was old, his sons were not walking in the paths of righteousness, and there was no open vision. The word of the Lord was rare in those days. But into the tabernacle had come a little boy consecrated to the Lord from his birth. His name was Samuel. "And it came to pass . . . before the lamp of God went out in the tabernacle of the Lord where the ark of God was, and while Samuel was lying down to sleep, that the Lord called Samuel. And he answered, 'Here I am!'" The Lord spoke to Samuel from off the mercy seat, and made known to him what was to befall the house of Eli. The chapter following reveals to us that judgment, and in it the ark is taken . . .

Prisoner of War (1 Sam. 4). The first verse says: "Now Israel went out to battle against the Philistines." The children of Israel are at fault. If the Philistines had declared war, it might have been another matter. God had not told them to go, and it was very soon seen that they were out of the will of God, for the battle went hard with them, four thousand being slain. They then thought of the ark of the Lord and said: "Let us bring the ark of the covenant of the Lord from Shiloh to us, that when it comes among us it may save us from the hand of our enemies" (1 Sam. 4:3). So the ark was carried to the battlefield, and when the soldiers saw it they raised a tremendous shout. As soon as the Philistines heard the shout they inquired the meaning of it, and when they heard that the ark of Israel's God had been brought they were afraid. The command was sent out: "Conduct yourself like men, and fight as you have never fought before!" The result was a great slaughter for Israel. Thirty thousand men were killed, including Hophni and Phinehas, the sons of Eli. Moreover, the ark of the covenant of the God of Israel was captured.

Eli, the old priest, was sitting on a seat awaiting news of the battle, for his heart trembled for the safety of the ark. When the messenger came from the battlefield, he told Eli the sad story of defeat and how his two sons were killed and the ark taken. At the news of the capture of the ark the old man of ninety-eight years fell from his seat and broke his neck. This now meant no priest, no successor to the priesthood, and no ark of God. Also, while the battle went amiss and as Phinehas was killed, back in the city his wife gave birth to a son. Upon hearing of the tragedies of the day and the loss of the ark and the priesthood, she named her newborn son *Ichabod*, meaning "The glory of the Lord has departed" (1 Sam. 4:21).

Oh! What tragedies come through disobedience! Instead of the nation following the God of ark, they planned their attack, made their arrangements, and then sought to bring the Lord into it as an afterthought, because things were difficult. Are we not often guilty of doing the same? We make our projects; we lay out our schemes for the running of a church, a mission, a campaign, this thing and that thing; and when we have done all, we call God in and ask Him to bless. May the dear Lord forgive us, and give us grace to follow Him and never ask Him to follow us, for it means utter failure and disappointment.

In the meantime, what happened to the ark? Did

the enemy now possess the power of God to use it against His chosen people? Let us see in our next chapter.

CHAPTER 21

The Journeyings of the Ark

2. From Philistia to the Temple

1 Samuel 5, 6, and 7. 2 Samuel 6 and 7. 1 Kings 8:1–11.
2 Kings 24 and 25. Revelation 11:19.

And it was told King David, saying, "The Lord has blessed the house of Obed-Edom and all that belongs to him, because of the ark of God." So David went and brought up the ark of God from the house of Obed-Edom to the City of David with gladness. And so it was, when those bearing the ark of the Lord had gone six paces, that he sacrificed oxen and fatted sheep. Then David danced before the Lord with all his might; and David was wearing a linen ephod. So David and all the house of Israel brought up the ark of the Lord with shouting and with the sound of the trumpet.

And as the ark of the Lord came into the City of David, Michal, Saul's daughter, looked through a window and saw King David leaping and whirling before the Lord; and she despised him in her heart. So they brought the ark of the Lord, and set it in its place in the midst of the tabernacle that David had erected for it. Then David offered burnt offerings and peace offerings before the Lord. And when David had finished offering burnt offerings and peace offerings, he blessed the people in the name of the Lord of hosts. Then he distributed among all the people, among the whole multitude of Israel, both the women and the men, to everyone a loaf of bread, a piece of meat, and a cake of raisins. So all the people departed, everyone to his house. (2 Sam. 6:12–19)

WE closed the last chapter wondering what the Philistines would do with the ark and how they would fare with it in their possession. Well, they wondered too! We find they treated it with the greatest of reverence and brought it into the . . .

Temple of Dagon at Ashdod (1 Sam. 5:2), and set it beside their idol god. They did not know what else to do with it. To them their temple was a holy place, but to God it was an abomination—for Scripture declares that God and mammon cannot dwell together. Something must happen, and something did happen. The next morning Dagon was found lying on his face on the floor. This caused much consternation among the Philistines as carefully they put the idol back into its place, wondering how such an accident had happened. The day following they learned that it was more than an accident, for there lay their god on the ground again, but this time with both his head and his hands broken off. He was reduced to a torso. Being headless, he could not think for them, see them or hear them; and having no hands, he could not work for them. To the Philistines, it must have been a great calamity.

But we are reminded of the fact that the presence of God means the downfall of idolatry. Many people today have helpless idols which they worship: friends, habits, or possessions that find first place in their life. When God comes in, in all the fullness of His power, these things go out as worthless. Verse 5 says: "Therefore neither the priests of Dagon nor any who come into Dagon's temple tread on the threshold of Dagon in Ashdod to this day."

The fall of Dagon was not the only strange thing that was happening, for a plague of tumors (symptoms, perhaps, of the bubonic plague) broke out in the city and many were dying. Therefore, they concluded that a curse was resting upon them and that the ark of the God of Israel was the cause; so they decided to send it away. It was taken to . . .

Gath (1 Sam. 5:8). But in that city the same plague broke out, and the hand of the Lord was very heavy against the people there. They therefore sent it away, and so it journeyed to . . .

Ekron (1 Sam. 5:10). Here, too, people raised an objection to the very approach of the ark, saying, "They have brought the ark of the God of Israel to us, to kill us and our people!" The plague was so severe that it was called a "deadly destruction."

Having endured seven months' suffering, not being willing to part with the evidence of a great "victory," the hour of necessity came when the . . .

Philistines Returned the Ark (1 Sam. 6). "But," said they, "do not send it empty, but return it with a trespass offering, that we may be healed." What could they send, for their worship differed from that of the Israelites? They decided, from their custom of giving to their god the representation of that from which they sought deliverance, to make five golden tumors and five golden rats—images of the rats that were ravaging the land. This is an inference of a further plague. Not only were the men smitten and Dagon overthrown, but the fields were also infested with rats which were destroying the crops.

They had prepared their trespass offering but they had no priesthood to carry the ark back to its place; so they built a new cart. No doubt it was fear and awe that made them so careful. Then there came a hesitation in their purposes. Suppose, after all, it was not a plague inflicted by the God of Israel, but just a strange coincidence. They would "put out their fleece" and so we have the . . .

Test of the Milk Cows (1 Sam. 6:7–12). They took two milk cows, two mothers that were with their young. The young were penned up while the mothers were hitched to the cart, with their heads turned toward Beth Shemesh where Israel was and their backs turned on their young. If the cows went straight ahead with the ark, "then the God of Israel has afflicted us," said the Philistines, but if the animals did what was the most natural thing for them to do—turn back when they heard the cry of their calves—then, said they, it was "not God." This was an unfair and unnatural test. But God can stand tests even if they are unnatural or contrary to nature. He is the God who had responded to Gideon with his fleece and, later, would consume with fire Elijah's water-saturated sacrifice. The glorious truth we behold in this incident is the willingness of God to return to a repentant people. If they will repent "I will heal their backsliding, I will love them freely . . ." (Hosea 14:4).

So the ark began its journey homeward, but it arrived only as far as . . .

Beth Shemesh (1 Sam. 6:12–21). The people there rejoiced and offered sacrifices. Later, however, the men of this city looked into the ark of the Lord. Whether it was out of concern for its entire safety or out of idle curiosity, we do not know, but it was a tremendous sin of presumption. In lifting the mercy seat they were lifting mercy from a law that they could not keep and so exposed themselves to the ministry of death. The result of that presumption was the death of seventy men. The people of Beth Shemesh would have no more to do with the ark and sent messengers to the next town, Kirjath Jearim, saying: "The Philistines have brought back the ark of the Lord; come down and take it up with you." So they came and carried the ark into the . . .

House of Abinadab in Kirjath Jearim (1 Sam. 7:1–2). The people of this place consecrated Eleazar, the son of Abinadab, to keep it. For twenty years the ark remained there, during which time the house of Abinadab was greatly blessed. All homes that have Christ dwelling in them are homes of blessing.

Doing a Right Thing in a Wrong Way (2 Sam. 6). In the course of time Saul was selected as Israel's king, and he was succeeded by David. David decided that he would have the ark brought up to Jerusalem. He gathered together thirty thousand chosen men and went down to Kirjath Jearim. The ark was put on another new cart which was driven by the sons of Abinadab, and once more, after a score of years, the journey home was resumed. David and the people accompanied the ark, playing on harps, lyres, tambourines, sistrums and cymbals. All went well until they came to . . .

Nachon's Threshingfloor (2 Sam. 6:6), where the ark toppled as the cart went over the rough floor and Uzzah reached out his hand to steady the ark—and dropped dead. How did such a tragedy happen? God had instructed that poles should be put to the ark that it might be borne with them, and that it should be carried on the shoulders of the priests. It was permissible for the Philistines to make a new cart, because they had no other means of conveying the ark. Had it been borne now in the prescribed way it would never have tottered.

What are the lessons to be learned? First, that Christ, of whom the ark is a type, is to be borne upon the shoulders and in the lives of the believers, who are priests unto God. The reason why the Church is in a condition of declension today is that men have been building their new carts—calling them new theology, modernism, higher criticism—and upon these carts they are seeking to fit Christ. The result has been a tottering and a falling in the Church, and some, like Uzzah, have had their faith destroyed as a result.

The second lesson comes from Uzzah, whom some have sought to excuse and justify; but, in seeking to justify a person whom God has punished, one is charging God with injustice. If the ark was typical of Christ—and it was—then a poor, weak man was putting forth his hand to uphold a falling Christ. This seems a shocking statement to make; but in practice this is what many are doing today. The Church is failing because it has put Christ onto carts of its own making, and to save it from failure—which men are attributing to the gospel instead of to themselves—they are seeking to support it by bingo games, dances, films, etc. What a tragic story!

The result of this experience was that the journey was once more delayed, and the ark was taken into the . . .

House of Obed-Edom (2 Sam. 6:10–11). There it remained for three months, while Obed-Edom also received blessing. How true it is that, while many churches are losing blessing, individuals and small communities are enjoying great blessing. At the end of three months the ark was . . .

Brought to Jerusalem (2 Sam. 6:12–19). This time it was carried in the correct way, on the shoulders of the priests, and with sacrifices and much national rejoicing. "So they brought the ark of the Lord, and set it in its place in the midst of the tabernacle that David had erected for it. Then David offered burnt offerings and peace offerings before the Lord." We must realize that this was the first time that the ark was brought to Jerusalem. When it was taken as the spoil of warfare twenty-one years previously, its place was then in Shiloh. But having come to the capital city, it was placed . . .

In a Tent (2 Sam. 7:2). At this time every man had his home, and the king his palace. They were no more pilgrims and strangers; they were in the land. Yet the ark had no permanency yet. It reminds one of the days when Christ was here in the flesh, and we read concerning Him: "And everyone went to his own house. But Jesus went to the Mount of Olives" (John 7:53–8:1). There He spent the night. He had nowhere to lay His head. Men had their homes, but not Jesus. You, my reader, have your home. You go to it, you enjoy its comforts, its rest, its protection. Have you thought of where Christ is to dwell? His place is in your heart. He desires to dwell in you richly, but He will not come in unless He is invited.

A Temple Built (2 Sam. 7 and 1 Kings 5 to 8). David desired to build a place worthy of God, and so said to Nathan the prophet, "See now, I dwell in a house of cedar, but the ark of God dwells inside tent curtains." But God said, "Would you build a house for Me to dwell in? For I have not dwelt in a house since the time that I brought the children of Israel up from Egypt, even to this day, but have moved about in a tent and in a tabernacle." David was not permitted to build that house but God accepted the desire and promised that his son would build a house for His name. That temple was eventually built by Solomon. The day of dedication arrived and the ark was brought to its . . .

Final Resting Place (1 Kings 8:1–11). "Now Solomon assembled the elders of Israel and all the heads of the tribes, the chief fathers of the children of Israel, to King Solomon in Jerusalem, that they might bring up the ark of the covenant of the Lord from the City of David, which is Zion. And all the men of Israel assembled to King Solomon at the feast in the month of Ethanim, which is the seventh month. Then all the elders of Israel came, and the priests took up the ark. And they brought up the ark of the Lord, the tabernacle of meeting, and all the holy furnishings that were in the tabernacle. The priests and the Levites brought them up. Also King Solomon, and all the congregation of Israel who were assembled to him, were with him before the ark, sacrificing sheep and oxen that could not be counted or numbered for multitude.

"Then the priests brought in the ark of the covenant of the Lord to its place, into the inner sanctuary of the temple, to the Most Holy Place, under the wings of the cherubim. For the cherubim spread their two wings over the place of the ark, and the cherubim overshadowed the ark and its poles. And the poles extended so that the ends of the poles could be seen from the holy place, in front of the inner sanctuary; but they could not be seen from outside. So they are there to this day. There was nothing in the ark except the two tablets of stone which Moses put there at Horeb, when the Lord made a covenant with the children of Israel, when they came out of the land of Egypt.

"And it came to pass, when the priests came out of the holy place, that the cloud filled the house of the Lord, so that the priests could not continue ministering because of the cloud; for the glory of the Lord filled the house of the Lord."

There the ark remained in its dwelling place.

The Temple Destroyed (2 Kings 24 and 25). In the destruction of the temple and Jerusalem under the hand of Nebuchadnezzar and the carrying away into Babylon, much of the temple is referred to, but nothing is said concerning the ark. It is never seen or heard of again. We can assume it was carried to Babylon, but what became of it there? We do not know. Some think it is hidden, others believe it will come to light again. But Jeremiah, prophesying concerning Israel's future said: " 'Then it shall come to pass, when you are multiplied and increased in the land in those days,' says the Lord, 'that they will say no more, "The ark of the covenant of the Lord." It shall not come to mind, nor shall they remember it, nor shall they visit it; nor shall it be made anymore' " (Jer. 3:16). This does not suggest a reappearance. I believe God in His own wonderful way removed that ark. We do not read, nor know anything, of its end. It has no end—so fulfilling its last and final type of Him who is eternal and who knows no end.

The ark has one more reference in Scripture.

The Ark in Heaven (Rev. 11:19). "Then the temple of God was opened in heaven, and the ark of His covenant was seen in His temple."

•   •   •

"See to it that you make it according to the pattern which was shown you on the mountain" was the instruction given to Moses. Here is the pattern. In type and in shadow we have meditated upon Christ and His Church. When we get to the "It is finished" of life and arrive in the glory land, we shall behold the "It is finished" of our salvation. For that ark is Christ!